television

THE FIRST FIFTY YEARS

telev

THE FIRST

Jeff

Harry N. Abrams, Inc

Greenfield

ision

FIFTY YEARS

Publishers, New York

For Carrie Carmichael
and for Casey Carmichael Greenfield:
the women in my life.

Editor: Lory Frankel
Designer: Nai Chang

Library of Congress Catalogue Card Number: 77-9159
International Standard Book Number: 0-8109-1651-7
© 1977 by Harry N. Abrams, B.V., The Netherlands

Contents

Preface and Acknowledgments

One of the limits on television advertising is a Federal Trade Commission prohibition against false and misleading claims. If a washday detergent gets out twice the dirt in half the time in a television commercial, it had better be able to prove that it can do it in a washing machine. If a gasoline promises more mileage with miracle ingredient X-567, there had better be an X-567.

So a word at the outset as to our intentions. More than offering a look back at television's visual past, this book attempts to explain some of what television has done over the first half-century of its life: how it developed, what has changed about it, what has remained constant, under what premises television has shaped its look and feel and content.

Many of these five hundred pictures will bring back fond recollections of old shows, performers from almost thirty years ago, as well as popular performers of today. These pictures, however, are here to illustrate some points about television programs, news, sports, advertising—and values. If we have had to choose between a picture that is fun to look at and a picture that helps explain something about the medium of television, we have usually chosen the latter. (Happily, we found that the pictures we had chosen provided ample fun on their own.)

We also met with an occasional failure in our attempt to provide an illustrated history of television's first fifty years. Some of the early days of television, broadcast live with no kinescopic recording, are gone forever. Many early programs on local stations that were recorded on kinescope have disappeared, because the stations did not realize the historical value of those kinescopes, and threw them out with yesterday's newspapers. Early television advertising is similarly difficult to document. In addition, copyright restrictions forced us to exclude some of what we wanted to show you.

What remains, however, is (immodestly) a remarkable collection of photographs, many of them never before put between book covers. They are here not just before put between book covers. They are here not just because they bring back memories, but because they *show* you what television is all about—how it reshaped American entertainment, politics, and marketing; how, in its assumptions about what we wanted to watch, and why, it helped to make those assumptions come true. And, as television has demonstrated so well, it is much more convincing to show an audience something than to tell it something.

In working on *Television: The First Fifty Years,* I came to understand something about why this device holds such a hypnotic spell on the great majority of Americans. The points I have tried to make in the text carry far more weight when they can be demonstrated "right in front of your eyes, ladies and gentlemen." Here you will see television taking hold of postwar America; you will see the remarkably consistent pattern in thirty years of television comedy; you will see televised drama change from the closeup character study to the slam-bang action-and-adventure film; you will see news and sports change from observers of events to their creators.

I hope you will enjoy this survey, but I hope also that you will learn from it—learn to understand how television searches for the biggest audience, the biggest payoff, the biggest impact. Like it or not, television is an instrument you must understand if you want to understand American society in the second half of the twentieth century. It is my hope that *Television: The First Fifty Years* will help you understand it a bit better.

Thank you for letting us into your living room.

It was our intention in this book to use the hundreds of photographs not simply to stir nostalgic memories among our readers, but to illustrate some of the themes of the text—to show, as well as to tell, what television is and how it has changed. This required an enormous amount of hard work, goodwill, and patience from the people at Harry N. Abrams, Inc., and from others who worked for us and with us.

To researchers Margaret Donovan, Susan Harris, and Anne Schotter, my thanks for a willingness to fight through the obscurity of my references and the unreliability of my unaided memory to find the facts. To photo researchers Linda Oken, Nancy Allen, Walter I. Seigal, and Pamela Rogow, my gratitude for their constant capacity to come up with the photographs that illustrated the point.

The public-information people at the major networks, who hold some of the most thankless jobs in the world, provided indispensable assistance. My thanks to Joe Riccuiti of NBC, New York; Earl Ziegler, Leona Blair, and Linda Hackley of NBC, Los Angeles; Rick Giacalone of ABC; and Mike Silvers and Joseph Belon of CBS. Fred Cantey of Associated Press's Wide World Photos, Inc., also rendered great assistance. My thanks as well to those too numerous to name or unknown to me at these companies and elsewhere who also worked so hard to help.

Four people at Harry N. Abrams deserve special thanks. Hugh Levin was in charge of the project from the beginning; he managed to maintain goodwill and good humor in the face of the author's frequent spells of demonic possession, and was both a thoughtful and careful judge of ideas and proposals.

Lory Frankel, who edited the text, is an author's nightmare and dream. Nightmare because her steely eye unfailingly found every unchallenged assumption, every insufficiently supported conclusion. At times she was single-handedly responsible for a bear market in the author's self-esteem. She is an author's dream because she helped to strengthen the book immeasurably, at the cost of sleep and relaxation. She has my special thanks.

Nai Chang, Abrams' art director, labored through last-minute deadlines and photo substitutions to design the format of this book. His contribution was invaluable.

Debra Feingold, the in-house photo researcher, thoughtfully refrained from hurling the author out of a seventh-story window upon receiving his frequent last-minute requests for twenty-five-year-old photos of long-dead shows. Instead, she almost always found what was needed.

Laurence Michie, who covers television for *Variety,* not only read the text and offered suggestions but also was a helpful source of facts and notions about the curious business of television.

Much as I would like to break with tradition and blame every error on these fine people, candor compels me to accept full responsibility for any errors of fact and judgment in the book.

Finally, to Carrie Carmichael and to Casey Carmichael Greenfield, my hopelessly inadequate appreciation for the missed weekends, the late nights, the dance recital unattended, and, most of all, for the sheer joy of sharing life with them.

TELEVISION COMES TO AMERICA

The Impact: What Television Has Done to America

Television is the pervasive American pastime, cutting through ethnic, class, and cultural diversity. It is the single binding thread of this country, the one experience that touches all of us . . .

Imagine yourself a stranger in an alien land, ignorant of its people, its customs, its values. How would you go about learning the nature of this civilization?

You would visit its marketplace, to see how goods and services are bought and sold.

You would visit its schools and playgrounds, to see how the young learn and how they play; and you would visit the elderly, to see how—and if—traditions are passed on to succeeding generations.

You would visit its forums, to hear how the concerns of the community are voiced, how they are resolved, how this civilization chooses its leaders.

You would seek out the teachers, to learn how the civilization learns about itself; you would attend ceremonies, to see what rituals define that society.

And you would seek to spend time in the homes of this civilization's people, to see what patterns of behavior unite them.

If an alien came to the shores of contemporary America, he could do all of this exploration through the use of television. And so powerful has television become that if he ignored it, he could not know how American civilization works.

With the single exception of the workplace, television is the dominant force in American life today. It is our marketplace, our political forum, our playground, and our school; it is our theater, our recreation, our link to reality, and our escape from it. It is the device through which our assumptions are reflected and a means of assaulting those assumptions.

Most starkly, television is the pervasive American pastime; cutting through geographic, ethnic, class, and cultural diversity, it is the single binding thread of this country, the one experience that touches young and old, rich and poor, learned and illiterate. A country too big for homogeneity, filled by people from all over the globe, without any set of core values, America never had a central unifying bond. Now we do. Now it is possible to answer the question, *"What does America do?"* We watch television.

For the first time in our history, it is possible to answer the question, "What does America do?" We watch television.

Whether it portrays reality or fantasy, television can trigger a national fashion change; *(opposite page)* Dorothy Hamill's gold medal in the 1976 Winter Olympics made "The Wedge" a popular hairstyle (and won Hamill an advertising contract with a hair-products company). Farrah Fawcett-Majors *(above)*, who began as a Noxzema Shaving Cream fantasy object, costarred in ABC's *Charlie's Angels*, which premiered in 1976. The show became a top-rated success, and the hairstyle a national trend.

Each year the numbers grow beyond credibility. At last count there were almost 116 million television sets in the United States: about one for every other American. And almost all of those sets are in operation more and more every year—at last count for an average of almost seven hours a day. However you look at these facts, their impact is staggering. Take all the hours worked by every American in a typical year of the early 1970s. It comes to about 2.8 billion hours. Take all the time spent by Americans watching television that same year. It comes to 1.5 billion hours. In coming years, as the number of older people rises and the size of the work force diminishes, the margin between those numbers will shrink. By the early twenty-first century, it is possible that we will watch television even more than we sleep or work. Already, a congressional report tells us, the average American spends one-fourth of his waking life watching television. And the only activity that takes up more of our children's time than watching television is sleeping.

No one who seeks to examine television can avoid the fact of its power. Those who work in television and those who study it may disagree about precisely *what* it does; but that it *does* hold unparalleled power over American life is indisputable. Speaking before a presidential commission on violence in the late 1960s, George Gerbner, Dean of the Annenberg School of Communications of the University of Pennsylvania, put it this way:

In only two decades of massive national existence television has transformed the political life of the nation, has changed the daily habits of our people, has moulded the style of the generation, made overnight global phenomena out of local happenings, redirected the flow of information and values from traditional channels into centralized networks reaching into every home. In other words it has profoundly affected what we call the process of socialization, the process by which members of our species become human.

Writer David Halberstam called television "an instrument that was, in both overt and subliminal ways, more important and dominant in our lives than newspapers, radio, church, and often, in the rootless America of the seventies, more important than family and more influential and powerful than the government itself."

Both the Left and the Right have perceived television to be a monumentally powerful political force; but, interestingly, each has seen it as an agent of its oppo-

One of the first television fads was the Davy Crockett frenzy, triggered by a film series that ran as part of *Disneyland* in 1955. More recent is the "Fonzie" phenomenon, which took off in the fall of 1975 when the *Happy Days* character, played by Henry Winkler, was elevated into a starring role. The faces of both Crockett and Fonzie adorned T-shirts, lunch boxes, comic books, and a wide range of profitable merchandise.

site. To the Left, television is a medium that perpetuates corporate control of America, using the seductive power of advertising to create artificial demands for wasteful, harmful products and supplying mind-numbing programs to act as a mid-twentieth-century version of Marx's "opiate of the masses." To the Right, it is a news medium dominated by voices hostile to traditional American values, celebrating upheaval and rebellion and encouraging dissent and even disloyalty against the presidency and America's national security. No one, it appears, sees in television a fair or accurate reflection of himself.

As for television's social impact, it is so pervasive that in the mid-1970s it is almost easier to list what social impact TV *hasn't* had. The medium, by its very reach, can alter the American idiom overnight. When *Laugh-In* was at its peak in 1968, the show resuscitated an old piece of material from black vaudeville days—a skit with the catchphrase, "Heah come de judge." Five days later, campaigning for the presidency, Robert Kennedy was met by placards and banners reading "Heah come de judge" at virtually every campaign stop he made. A massively successful entertainment show—particularly one that reaches large numbers of children and adolescents—can send a phrase such as "up your nose with a rubber hose" (in *Welcome Back, Kotter*) from obscurity into the national slang by the very act of repetition. From the days of the Davy Crockett-coonskin-cap fad of 1955 to the Fonzie and Bionic Woman craze of the mid-seventies, television has become the all-but-exclusive creator and director of our children's enthusiasms.

But these are trivial powers compared to the broader reach of this medium. It has altered the eating and sleeping habits of most Americans. It has kept them up later at night: but it has also kept them home, seeking entertainment and recreation in the privacy of their living rooms instead of in company at movie theaters, nightclubs, or social gatherings. (This impact seems to have escaped the attention of even the most powerful of television's power brokers. In the mid-1960s, Columbia Broadcasting System founder and board chairman William Paley devoted himself to a restaurant in the new CBS building. When it was failing, he asked his manager if it should try to reach a late-night supper-club clientele. "Bill," the manager said, "there ain't no supper business in this town. Everybody's home watching the tube.") It has broken the traditional patterns of how we learn about the world as children; of how we decide who shall gain our votes for national leadership; of how we identify ourselves. Children may well learn more from television than from their parents, who depend on television as a source of diversion for their children. Voters no longer need to rely on the machinery of the political clubhouse or party to convey information about candidates, because those candidates now reach the voter directly, powerfully, "face to face" through television. And without the need to rely on political parties, the rise of the independent voter—who chooses on the basis of character and personality rather than party affiliation—has become a central fact of postwar American political life.

Television has altered the shape and speed of our knowledge of the world, and in so doing has far outstripped its onetime competitors—has even, in several instances, obliterated them. In the 1930s, even as network radio grew, the mass-circulation magazine was a centerpiece of American life, both for learning the news of the world (*Life*) and for escaping from it (the *Saturday Evening Post*). But by the time network television was little more than twenty-five years old, the four dominant weekly mass magazines—*Life, Look, Collier's*, and the *Saturday Evening Post*—had all died. And the most widely circulated magazine in the United States was, of course, *TV Guide*. Television had become at once the dominant medium of mass commercial fiction and the dominant medium of mass factual information. And at times neither the producers nor consumers of television knew where the values of the one stopped and the values of the other began.

The sheer power and reach of this medium is one reason why we understand so little about it. Another, often neglected, reason is that television contains within itself a remarkable collection of paradoxes:

• It is called a medium of communication, but it lacks a critical element of communication as found in the telephone, telegraph, or speech: it only reaches one way. Writer Robert Lewis Shayon has noted perceptively that broadcasting is, in fact, the transmission of a *simultaneous message to anonymous multitudes*. The "communicator" on television literally has no idea who he is talking to.

• Television is a visual medium, but unlike a painting, a sculpture, or even a movie, it purveys totally transitory data. Many of the most widely shared experiences of our society have come through the viewing of moments in history which none of us has ever seen again. Despite the existence of old kinescopes and contemporary

As early as 1949, American families were discovering that television could exert a magnetic charm, replacing outmoded mealtime traditions such as conversation.

The historic Paramount Theater in Times Square, New York City, fell to the wrecker's ball in 1967. Throughout American cities, the big, downtown movie palaces came down: victims of the television era.

When ABC began telecasting Dick Clark's *American Bandstand* in 1957, it not only made instant folk heroes out of South Philadelphia teenagers, but made new dances national fads overnight. "The Stroll" and "the Jerk" were duplicated in high school gyms across America days after they were introduced on this after-school show.

Television shows could offer news and a friendly group of reassuring faces from dawn until midnight. The *Today* show has been doing it successfully for twenty-five years. This 1958 edition features Jack Lescoulie, Charles Van Doren (shortly before the quiz show investigations revealed his part in the rigging), Betsy Palmer, Frank Blair, and Dave Garroway, the first of the show's hosts.

video tapes our experience of television is immediate—reinforced for historical events or spectacular touchdown catches through instant replay—and then gone forever.

• Television has made the once inaccessible familiar, but it has made the familiar less attractive. In the early days of television, celebrities would thank the audience for "letting us come into your living room at night," and that sense of familiarity has always charac-

terized the medium. Newscasters, talk-show hosts, actors in daytime dramas find themselves treated as neighbors on the streets of a strange community, hailed on a first-name basis, approached almost cheerfully, barriers already surmounted by constant exposure. At the same time, Americans have withdrawn from their communal experiences—the church, the civic club, the neighborhood—because they do not need them anymore for diversion or a sense of connection to the outside world. "In living color more real than life," TV historian Erik Barnouw has written, "the swirling dots represent the world ... they have become the environment and context of our lives." And as early as the mid-1950s, says American historian Eric Goldman, "for many Americans home was close to meaning the place where the TV set was located." And those who inhabited our homes were less and less our children, parents, spouses, or friends. They were those who informed, entertained, amused, diverted us from inside the picture tube. Home was less and less the place where we gathered to talk to each other when the day was done, more and more the place we sat watching others talk—from dawn (*Today, Good Morning, America*) through daylight and dusk (*Dinah!, The Mike Douglas Show*) to dark (*The Tonight Show,* with Johnny Carson).

We had always known that television, when it came, would be a medium of great power. One American observer, E. B. White, worried publicly about the impact of television in a 1938 essay:

> Television will enormously enlarge the eye's range, and, like radio, will advertise the Elsewhere . . . A door closing heard over the air, a face contorted, seen in a panel of light—these will emerge as the real and the true—and when we bang the door of our own cell, or look into another face the impression will be of mere artifice.

But for American society, television was distinctly a postwar phenomenon. Indeed, its swift conquest of America can be linked in large measure to the fact that television as an instrument reflected one of the populace's most insistent desires after World War II—to be left alone. Throughout that war, Americans had been pushed together—into barracks and into assembly plants, into overcrowded trains and buses (autos were left behind, thanks to gas rationing), into lines at grocery stores and induction centers and hotels. They had all come together for a great national effort; and the central promise of the propaganda of the day was that when it was over, they would all enjoy a life of splendid, affluent privacy, with their own corner of the world in the suburbs and the comfort of their own automobile.

Television was one more marvel by which Americans could retreat into their own lives. In 1946, there were 7,000 television sets in use throughout America. In 1947, 178,000 more were manufactured and the au-

New York's Astor Hotel lobby was packed in October, 1944; so were hotel lobbies across the country; so were trains and planes, army barracks and assembly plants. Americans had been crowded together all through World War II. Now they wanted some space. They wanted to be left alone. And television was the perfect kind of entertainment to satisfy that urge.

These crowds are gathered at the Boston Common to watch the 1948 World Series on television. But though the setting is a common, the vision of television is decidedly private.

The first experience with television, ironically, was usually communal, standing in front of appliance-store windows, or scratching for a place at the bar to watch the 1947 World Series live, direct from Yankee Stadium.

dience was estimated at 1 million, mostly in the East. In 1948, Milton Berle began his run on the National Broadcasting Company, and New York theater and restaurant owners noticed a collapse in business at 8 P.M. on Tuesday nights. That year, 975,000 TV sets were manufactured. A year later, more than 3 million were made. In May, 1950, Baltimore became the first city where more hours were spent watching television than listening to the radio. A year later, the Kefauver crime hearings were fed to stations around the eastern half of the country. In January, 1952, television's dominant share of American leisure habits became a national fact for the first time. We had begun by experiencing television as a more or less communal phenomenon—in bars, in exhibition halls, standing outside hardware stores watching the World Series, crowding into the house of a pioneering neighbor. In the early 1950s, by the millions, we took television into

Soon, however, Americans were safe at home, enjoying television as it was meant to be seen.

In the fall of 1952, Senator Richard Nixon, the Republican vice-presidential candidate, went before the television cameras to explain an $18,000 "slush fund" used to supplement expense allowances. He didn't talk to a crowd but to the viewers, face to face. He evoked his wife's "respectable Republican cloth coat," and "admitted" taking as a gift from a supporter—a little dog named Checkers. His children loved the dog, Nixon said, and he resolved not to give it back. It was a political triumph, and a clear signal that politicians had a new way of talking to the voter.

our homes and closed the door behind us.

In time, this retreat would level the great movie palaces of an earlier age, and the late-night supper clubs of the central cities. It would alter the look of motion pictures; the one demand television could not—or would not—supply was a franker look at sex. So Hollywood, which once had production codes forbidding double beds, and which once fought a major battle over using the word "virgin" in a movie, removed virtually all taboos against language and sexuality on film.

Television also altered the look of newsstands. In the mid-1950s, *Playboy* began the nudity revolution. Its success was due in large measure to the growing obsolescence of the mass-circulation magazine. Readers could get news more quickly and completely on television than in still photographs; they could not get pictures of naked women. The trend was clear; by the mid-1970s, magazine covers were more explicit than the first *Playboy* centerfold had been.

Beyond the treatment of sex, print publications discovered that television had simply overwhelmed the mass market. The key to survival now lay in specialization—in looking for the subcultures that television was too big to reach. And from *Mad* magazine to *New York*, from *Scientific American* to *Rolling Stone,* from the *Village Voice* to the *Star*, from *People* to *Money*, publications survived and flourished precisely because they worked against the frame of reference of television. Assuming their readers' reliance on television for the look and feel of American life, these publications tried to tell the readers how to survive in that life, or what was happening in the corners of that life television could not reach, or what was *really* going on behind the facile neutrality of TV news.

Television also altered the political process, and not just by the fact of its presence as a new way of reaching voters. The smarter politicians understood that television did not simply point its cameras at reality and transmit it—television *was* reality. As early as 1952, Republican candidate Eisenhower was using one-minute spots, while Democrat Stevenson was buying half-hour time periods to declaim in front of mass audiences. But making speeches in front of crowds does not exploit the medium; television is a means of talking to millions of voters *one or two at a time*. In 1952, Richard Nixon sat in a homey living-room–style set and spoke of his wife's cloth coat and his daughters' puppy dog. It enraged his opponents, but it worked. And eight years later, Nixon was a victim of the same principle. In their televised debate, Nixon had talked to the studio audience and to his opponent, while John Kennedy went straight for the camera and the mass audience. That critical first debate was more than a matter of Richard Nixon's pallor, or makeup, or shirt collar. It was absolute evidence that reality was what reached the living rooms of millions of anonymous voters—*not* what actually happened outside a factory gate. The images of candidates, built up in the past by partisan newspapers or campaign songs and buttons, were now subject to the individual judgment of every voter in the country.

The politicians understood this very well. From John Kennedy on, presidents of the United States took a persistent, sometimes obsessive interest in what television was saying about them. Kennedy used television to ram home his hold on the office after a razor-thin election by becoming the first president to permit live telecast of presidential news conferences. Lyndon Johnson moved the time of major addresses, such as the State of the Union address, to prime time at night, and kept three monitors in the Oval Office to watch the

The same Richard Nixon who had been saved by television in 1952 was undone by it in 1960, when in his first debate with Senator John F. Kennedy, Nixon appeared pale, tense, nervous. Lighting and makeup were two prominently named culprits, and in 1964, an NBC makeup man demonstrated how he'd use his skills to improve the Nixon image.

Five days after his inauguration in 1961, President Kennedy became the first chief executive to permit live television coverage of his press conferences. (He's shown here at a press conference in August of that year.) Kennedy's wit, good looks, and political understanding of television enabled him to shore up his public acceptability after the narrowest presidential victory of the twentieth century.

Spiro Agnew, here being interviewed by CBS's Mike Wallace at the 1968 Republican Convention, became the point man in the most sustained attack mounted on the television networks by any administration. Agnew's 1969 Des Moines speech, attacking network news for both bias and concentration of power, began a conflict between the Nixon administration and television that went on until Agnew resigned under fire in 1973 and Nixon resigned under threat of impeachment in 1974.

evening news. But he never trusted himself enough to employ the one technique that might have saved his presidency in the wake of Vietnam and domestic upheaval: when he spoke on television, he always strove to maintain a formal, dignified posture. (It took Jimmy Carter in 1976 to show how successfully television could be used by a deliberately informal presence.)

And when Richard Nixon came to the White House—fully conscious of the way televised images of Vietnam, cities in flames, conventions in upheaval, and campuses in disarray had helped erode confidence in Lyndon Johnson—his administration moved early to shore up support by discrediting what they saw as an untrustworthy medium. The assaults by the Nixon White House, and by Vice-President Spiro Agnew in particular, were stark testimony to two facts: first, television had become the overwhelming center of the American "polity"—that mechanism through which matters of public concern are debated and resolved. Second, large numbers of Americans harbored an essential mistrust of the medium—as if, after twenty years, we were still unsure of what it was that had occupied our living rooms all this time. Polls would show a high degree of trust in television; by the mid-seventies almost two-thirds of Americans were relying on it as their principal source of news, and almost half of all Americans trusted it more than any other source of information. Yet whenever television touched a sensitive subject—the civil-rights movement, the war in Vietnam, student dissent, crime, gun control—there were charges that television was not covering reality but was distorting it; that television was not a window on the world but a series of fun-house mirrors, deliberately designed to portray America falsely.

And yet, public figures were no more able to ignore the power of this medium—whatever their feelings about it—than they would be able to confine their efforts to persuasion by mental telepathy. Television had reformulated the classic hypothesis of Bishop Berkeley; today, if a tree fell in the forest and it wasn't on the six o'clock news, it might as well not have fallen at all. So the distrustful Richard Nixon used television more intensively than any of his predecessors to speak to the people directly—in an attempt to overcome the very distortions he believed television caused. Ralph Nader might see television as a pacifier, standing between citizens and a mass movement for reform, but he used television skillfully. He sought to modify his "goody-two-shoes" image by appearing on a *Dean Martin Celebrity Roast*, as well as the aggressively irreverent *Saturday Night*. Politi-

The power of television to blur distinctions between well-known people—to incorporate them all under the "celebrity" banner—has been strengthened by the willingness of public figures to gain publicity by crossing over once firm boundaries. Heavyweight fighter Muhammad Ali *(left)*, once notorious as a draft resister, is just one of the guys on a *Dean Martin Celebrity Roast*. Then-New York Mayor John Lindsay chats with Johnny Carson, Bill Cosby, and Ed McMahon on *The Tonight Show (below)*. Hubert Humphrey shows Dinah Shore how to cook a favorite meal on *Dinah! (below, left)*, and then-First Lady Betty Ford puts in a cameo appearance on *The Mary Tyler Moore Show (bottom)*.

A creature of television's insatiable desire for the new, the different, the quirky, Tiny Tim exchanged marriage vows with "Miss Vicky," on *The Tonight Show* in December, 1969.

As television changed our perception of the world, it altered our expectations as well. Now it was not enough to *be* at an event; we expected the same up-close access we had at home. This 1953 Academy Award audience sees Bob Hope the way they expect to—through a giant television screen close-up. Over the years, arenas did the same for performances of major rock stars, and sports complexes began installing giant television screens to show instant replays.

cians from John Lindsay to Hubert Humphrey to Ronald Reagan sought to use the medium to project a sense of warmth and friendliness, and often found themselves in the no-man's-land between information and entertainment offerings. Authors with messages of injustice and oppression, impending catastrophes, and environmental dangers found themselves sandwiched in between cabaret stars and comedians, and accepted that position willingly—because ten minutes in one of America's surrogate salons would bring their message to more Americans than a lifetime of lectures. (Whether what they had to say penetrated

the effect of the surroundings is another question.)

Finally, television over the last twenty-five years began to alter another important part of American life—television itself. The medium indeed began as an observer, placing its cameras in front of a group of actors, or a baseball game, or a Senate committee, or a convention. But the more powerful it grew, the more it began to reshape itself—and that which it covered—to the imperatives of the visual demands. Political conventions moved their sessions toward the evening hours to capture larger audiences, and placards and podiums were redesigned to look as good as possible.

So casual, so intimate was our sense of these daily television visitors that they became as important a part of our lives as the shows themselves, even when the shows were news reports about world leaders. Barbara Walters, here hosting a 1976 NBC special on "Children of Divorce," created national headlines when she moved to ABC in 1976—for a reported million dollars a year—to become the first regular anchor*woman* on a network news show. On her first special, in between visits to the homes of Barbra Streisand and Jimmy Carter, Walters took the viewer on a tour of another home—hers.

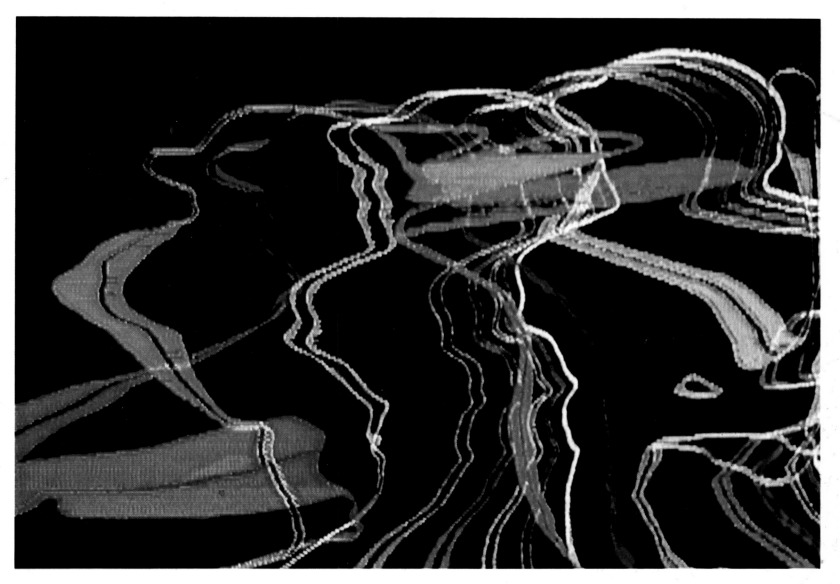

The world of sports became colorful, fragmented, a prime arena for the display of television's technical wonders, including computer animation to provide excitement for the viewer before the event even began.

The original attraction of television drama—a close-up look at people in conflict—was replaced by an obsession with action. The imperative of swift movement, symbolized for television's critics by the car chase and the explosion, still dominates much of prime-time television drama. The camera was no longer content to watch sports events; it enhanced them, by slowing down the action, isolating it, repeating it, giving the home audience a view that no spectator on the scene could hope for—to the point where the most modern sports arenas featured giant television screens for the benefit of those who paid to attend in person.

In sports, as well as in news and entertainment, the personalities of the performers proved to be an irresist-

ible magnet. Both in their camera work and in their subjects, television programs began to focus, in the words of an ABC Sports feature, "Up Close and Personal." Television made whoever was on the screen a central focus; so that Walter Cronkite or Barbara Walters or Howard Cosell came to overwhelm the subjects they were talking about. Viewers not only saw a quarterback throwing a pass or a skier breaking a world jumping record, but they were taken into athletes' homes, into the bosoms of their families, in a relentless search for intimacy.

And in the world of advertising, the limitless visual possibilities of television—to dazzle, to attract, to sell—came to be tapped more than in the programs

Neither the motion picture industry nor live entertainment like the circus was any match for a medium that could bring history right to our doorsteps. These circus performers *(right)* are watching General Douglas MacArthur's speech to a joint session of Congress in 1951; on the set of the movie *High Noon*, Gary Cooper, Grace Kelly, and the rest of the cast watch a World Series game of the same year.

themselves. Investing enormous amounts of time, money, and effort, advertisers in the 1960s turned television from a simple medium of show and tell into a medium of explosive colors, graphics, jump cuts, experimental photography—which in turn influenced everything from packaging to clothing fashions to the look of TV programming itself.

It was a fitting kind of influence. For in its thirty years

of wide-scale national use, in its fifty years of technological existence, television had come to touch every other part of our national existence, to stand with the automobile as one of the two transforming devices of American life, to stand alone in the range and reach of its influence. It *is* our society as is no other institution; it was to be expected that it should find itself changing shape under its own impact.

Form and Function: How Television Took Shape

These sketches from an 1882 series by French artist Albert Robida offer a prophetic look at television and its potential uses, some of which still have not come to pass. At home Parisians "enjoy" a desert battle; a lady of the house selects fabrics through the miracle of television; a ballerina, chorus, and orchestra are brought directly into the home of a relaxed viewer; and an adult education course is conducted long-distance.

Television must stand as one of the least surprising inventions in human history.

Within a few years of Alexander Graham Bell's public demonstration of the telephone in 1876, television had become a subject for popular artists such as George Du Maurier and Albert Robida. They depicted its use in everything from interoffice communication to coverage of foreign wars. With Samuel Morse's telegraph and Bell's telephone extending instant human communication across great distances, the idea of communicating by pictures was a natural next step. More important, the first steps toward transmitting images were taken within a decade of the development of the telephone. And while those images at first required transmission by wire, the relative ease of turning images into electrical impulses would make television broadcasting an absolute certainty as soon as the voice was liberated from the wire by Guglielmo Marconi at the end of the nineteenth century.

There is no one inventor, no one conceptual breakthrough that can be said to have marked the beginning of television. The medium owes much to Morse and Bell for grasping the communications potential of electric impulses. In 1884, a twenty-four-year-old German named Paul Nipkow developed a mechanical scanning device called the Nipkow disk. This disk was perforated with thousands of tiny holes. When it was rotated in front of a focused image of an object, the holes permitted bits of light and dark to pass through in rapid succession. A photoelectric cell converted each bit of light into an electrical impulse. A similarly perforated disk in the receiver, rotating exactly in step with the first disk, reproduced the object on a viewing screen by reconverting the electric current to the original pattern of lights and darks. But without radio signals or the coaxial cable, there was no way to carry the image over great distances, and even at short distances the image reproduction was poor.

Radio pioneers Guglielmo Marconi and Lee De Forest provided two critical elements in the birth of television: Marconi by liberating communication from

From 1884 until the 1920s, the only workable device for breaking an image down and converting it into electrical impulses was a mechanical scanning device known as the "Nipkow disk," named after its inventor, Paul Nipkow. This model was used by General Electric in a series of experiments of the 1920s. The bulk and complexity of the device, as well as the poor quality of the picture, led to attempts to supplant the mechanical device with a more efficient, all-electronic scanning system.

In 1927, Secretary of Commerce Herbert Hoover and American Telephone and Telegraph President Walter Gifford exchanged conversational pleasantries along a Washington-to-New York television hookup. An AT&T spokesman explains the mechanical scanning device enabling these pictures to appear on the 2½-inch screens.

The April, 1911, issue of *Modern Electrics*, edited by science-fiction pioneer Hugo Gernsback, featured the opening section from a prophetic novel, *Ralph 124C 41 +*. It also featured an article about the transmission of visual images along telephone lines, through a device called "the Telephot."

the wire (with an assist from Reginald Aubrey Fessenden, who used his voice instead of code); and De Forest by inventing the "Audion" tube, a glass bulb that captured and greatly amplified radio waves, providing the key to clarity. And even while the concept of television was still linked to the mechanical scanner, experiments were going on all through the first three decades of the twentieth century in television transmission.

As early as 1907, the magazine *Scientific American* used the word "television" to describe the transmission of pictures. In 1910, the Kansas City *Times* told its readers that "television [is] on the way" in its report on French experiments in the new medium. A year later, in his magazine *Modern Electrics*, Hugo Gernsback used the word "television" to describe visual telephones. In 1925, John L. Baird in England gave the first public demonstration of a television system. Charles Francis Jenkins followed him with the first telecast of an object in motion in June of that year. In April of 1927, Secretary of Commerce Herbert Hoover and American Telephone and Telegraph President Walter S. Gifford exchanged pleasantries in the first

Dr. E. F. W. Alexanderson (right) and Ray D. Kell pose here with an RCA mechanical scanner in 1927, shortly before the work of Philo T. Farnsworth and Vladimir Zworykin made such devices obsolete.

public demonstration of intercity television by wire, appearing on two-and-a-half-inch screens. A year later, station WRNY in Coytesville, New York, became the first regular broadcast station to transmit a television image. On May 11 of that year, General Electric began the first regular television broadcast schedule over station WGY in Schenectady, New York.

But none of these systems provided an alternative to the mechanical scanner, which was difficult to synchronize, noisy, bulky, vulnerable to breakdown, and which produced dim, fuzzy images. Boris Rosing, in 1905, and A. A. Campbell-Swinton, in 1911, had proposed the use of electronic means to transmit and receive television pictures, but they never put their

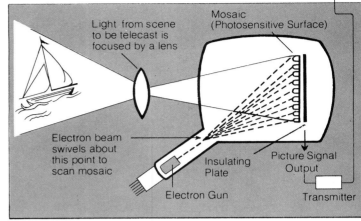

Master Antenna

Light from scene to be telecast is focused by a lens

Mosaic (Photosensitive Surface)

Electron beam swivels about this point to scan mosaic

Insulating Plate

Electron Gun

Picture Signal Output

Transmitter

These two men perfected the all-electronic television system, which displaced the mechanical scanner. Philo T. Farnsworth *(below)*, developed the "dissector tube," an electronic alternative to the mechanical disassembling and reassembling of pictures, and Vladimir K. Zworykin *(left)*, developed the iconoscopic camera and the kinescopic receiving tube. These devices made it possible to transmit and receive television pictures instantaneously, through the use of electrical signals.

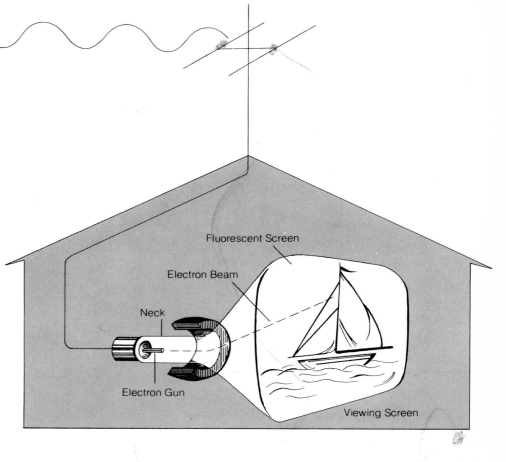

theories into practice. Two men—Philo T. Farnsworth and Vladimir Zworykin—broke television free from the limits of the mechanical scanner by creating an all-electronic system: one that could capture a visual image, convert it into electrical impulses, and then restore it, clearly and sharply, as a visual image.

Farnsworth, a young American engineer, scrapped the mechanical disk in favor of a cathode ray (he called it a dissector tube), which electronically "scanned" the visual image, and reproduced it far more clearly than a mechanical scanner could. (He applied for his patent in 1927, at the age of twenty-one, was granted the patent in 1930, and ultimately forced the giant Radio Corporation of America to break its ironclad rule and pay royalties to an outside inventor.) Zworykin, working independently as an engineer for Westinghouse, developed his own electronic system, the iconoscopic camera and the kinescopic tube, which opened the door to television as a mass medium. These inventions formed the basis for what we know as television.

Their premise is that the television image is an optical illusion in the same sense that the film image is an optical illusion. Film, of course, does not really present a moving image. Instead, it presents a number of still photographs each second—24 frames each second in modern film—which move too quickly for the human eye to notice. To us, it appears as a "moving picture."

Television relies on a similar frailty of the human eye. The television camera "reads" a visual image as dots of varying intensity, according to their brightness. This image, as dots of light, is focused through the camera lens onto a photosensitive surface, composed of minute elements. As light hits these elements, photoelectrons are released. An electron gun then scans the photosensitive surface at great speed, from left to right in alternate lines. It reads the odd-numbered lines first, at 1/60 of a second, then returns to read the even-numbered lines, also at 1/60 of a second (this is known as interlaced scanning). As the electron gun moves over the photosensitive surface, it causes an electrical current to flow from each element, each communicating one element of the picture as an electrical impulse. The electron gun in the television camera sends the broken-down image (the video signal) to the transmitter; there, the signal is amplified to the proper frequency level and then sent to an antenna which broadcasts it through the air in the form of radio waves. The signal is picked up by the home antenna, changed back to the frequency of the camera, and relayed to an electron gun in the receiver which is synchronized with the electron gun in the camera. The electron gun in the televi-

In March, 1950, an international group of scientists, technicians, and government officials met in New York to discuss how to make television transmission standard around the world. It never happened. Most European television operates on a scanning system of 625 lines at 25 frames per second, while American television uses 525 at 30 frames per second. The greater number of lines of the European system provides a better picture.

sion set throws the image onto the television screen. The fluorescent screen converts the photoelectrons back into visible dots of light.

What we are really looking at when we watch television is a 262 1/2-line image lasting 1/60 of a second, followed by a separate 262 1/2-line image lasting another 1/60 of a second. If the human eye worked as quickly as a fast-action camera, we could actually see these two separate "half-pictures." But since the human eye "retains" images far longer, we instead "see" a complete 525-line image, totally re-created every 1/30 of a second.

(Color television adds to this process red, blue, and green filters that scan gradations of color.)

These technical matters are often overlooked by those who view television as a social, political, or cultural instrument. Yet throughout the development of broadcasting as a force of unparalleled power in American life, technical matters have had a way of determining crucially important aspects of television and radio—how they grew, who ran them, who paid for them and how, and what the audience had a chance to see and hear. In this sense, the famous architectural dictum of Louis H. Sullivan has to be stood on its head. As far as broadcasting in America is concerned, function followed form.

Consider the growth of commercial radio broadcasting, the foundation on which television in America was grafted virtually without debate. Marconi had turned his radio invention into a business venture with the formation of a British corporation in 1897. Two years later, the Marconi Wireless Company of America, known as "American Marconi," was incorporated in New Jersey. (It was a twenty-one-year-old employee of this company—wireless operator David Sarnoff—who, legend has it, received the first word of the sinking of the Titanic in 1912. His reported seventy-two-hour vigil, receiving and relaying news of the disaster, made American Marconi and Sarnoff world famous.) When World War I broke out, the U.S. Navy immediately grasped the enormous military potential of radio, and urged the development of a radio monopoly in American hands—if not governmental, then private. Out of this pressure, and out of private discussions between the navy and General Electric, was born the Radio Corporation of America. Incorporated in October, 1919, RCA limited itself to American directors and officers, and because the United States government controlled the radio land stations, British-owned American Marconi was in effect forced to transfer all its assets and liabilities to the new American company. The Radio

(above) Guglielmo Marconi, inventor of "wireless" radio (right), and David Sarnoff, president of the Radio Corporation of America, pose on a visit to RCA's "radio central" in 1933. (below) Sarnoff gained national fame at the age of twenty-one by being the only wireless operator to maintain contact with the scene of the Titanic disaster in 1912.

Corporation of America began as a joint venture of four enormously powerful private companies: GE, Westinghouse, United Fruit, and AT&T. These companies did not organize in order to create a programming giant. AT&T wanted to insure the dominance of its transmission lines; GE and Westinghouse envisioned a huge market in the manufacture and sale of radio receivers. David Sarnoff, who came to RCA from American Marconi, saw the supply of programs as a stimulant to the sale of radio receivers.

Thus, very early in the world of radio broadcasting, four separate corporations with complementary concentrations of economic power virtually dominated the new medium, and each moved into this uncharted area with a specific collection of assumptions created by technology. For example, Western Electric, a subsidiary of AT&T, was incensed by the proliferation of transmitters in the early 1920s, most of which were manufactured by rivals of the company. RCA—owned in substantial measure by AT&T—began a series of suits against these competitors on the grounds of patent infringement.

More significantly, AT&T decided in 1922 to operate radio as it had telephones: i.e., to charge a fee to anyone who cared to come into a broadcasting "telephone booth" and broadcast a message to the growing world of radio listeners. The idea of financing broadcasts by commercials was considered an outrage by everyone from Secretary of Commerce Hoover to RCA General Manager Sarnoff, who proposed that programming be financed by an excise tax on receivers (the method most European nations still use to finance broadcasting). But AT&T was interested in applying the frame of reference of telephone financing to its new technology, as indicated in their term for commercials—"toll broadcasting." So, on August 28, 1922, when an executive of the Queensboro Corporation entered AT&T's station WEAF in New York and broadcast, for one hundred dollars, a ten-minute ode to the joys of owning an apartment in Long Island's Jackson Heights, it was not seen as the dawn of commercial, advertiser-supported broadcasting. It was simply a customer walking into the facility of a "common carrier"—a neutral transmitter of messages—and sending a message for a fee.

(That first commercial was a forebear of what was to come. "Let me enjoin you," said the spokesman, "as you value your health and your hopes and your home happiness, get away from the solid masses of brick, where the meager opening admitting a slant of sunlight is mockingly called a light shaft, and where children grow up starved for a run over a patch of grass and the sight of a tree." Even then, broadcast advertising was not excessively modest in its prose.)

But when entrepreneurs discovered that eager radio listeners would absorb a commercial message as readily as any other broadcast sound, and department stores found the curious flocking to their stores simply to observe radio broadcasting in action, these businessmen saw the clear capacity of the medium to draw huge numbers of potential customers. AT&T began toll broadcasting with the assumption that the telephone industry would provide the model for financing radio. But its experiment brought completely different results. Broadcasting was limited to those with sufficient financial incentive and resources to pay for the chance to reach great numbers of people. The airwaves in the early 1920s had been filled with the voices of hopeful amateurs and individuals with a desire to be heard. By the end of the decade, radio had become a mass medium from which the mass of people were almost completely excluded—except as listeners and consumers.

The explosive growth of radio broadcasting and the need to bring technical order into the field created the structure of government regulation that has endured for half a century. In 1926, an Illinois District Court held that there was no federal law to permit the secretary of commerce to assign station licenses. Congress moved quickly to provide such authority. In 1927, it passed the Radio Act and established the Federal Radio Commission. This law, designed to establish order by confining radio stations to specific broadcasting frequencies, also established the relationship between government and broadcaster that carried over almost unchanged into the regulation of television.

It provided for limited licenses to broadcasters: it specifically did *not* confer the ownership of airwaves to broadcasters. It required licensees to serve "the public interest, convenience or necessity." In a legislative inconsistency that is still with us, the Radio Commission was forbidden to act as a censor but was required to determine periodically whether the station was in fact serving the public interest.

In 1934, recognizing that broadcasting would soon come to encompass more than radio, Congress passed the Communications Act. The Radio Commission became the Federal Communications Commission, but the essential structure of broadcasting—private corporations operating for profit on government-licensed airwaves—remained unchanged.

The growth of the broadcasting network was also

In 1921, David Sarnoff (first row, second from left), showed off an RCA transoceanic station at New Brunswick, New Jersey, to a group of scientists. The man near the center, with the wide-brimmed hat and dark moustache, is Albert Einstein. The undersize man in the middle is Charles Steinmetz, a General Electric scientist whose work on alternating current opened the way for its widespread application.

structured by technological pressures. In the 1920s, AT&T—which claimed for itself the sole right to charge "tolls" for broadcasting—began to supply radio programs along its transmission lines. Its rivals in the fledgling business—RCA, General Electric, and Westinghouse—found that there were no alternative lines they could use for broadcasting. What had begun as a combine was developing into a life-and-death struggle between AT&T and its one-time partners in the creation of RCA. When AT&T indicated its interest in manufacturing and marketing radio receivers, the dispute became a full-fledged corporate war. Ultimately, through the pressures of the antitrust laws and a lengthy and complex battle fought out in the courts, regulatory agencies, and closed-door negotiations, AT&T withdrew from the broadcasting business in return for a guarantee that radio would use its transmission lines exclusively. And, in September of 1926, RCA formed the National Broadcasting Company—the first full-fledged broadcasting network.

It was the technological basis of broadcasting, however—the sending of a radio signal through the air which could be picked up only within a limited radius— that made network broadcasting necessary in the first place. Today there are numerous alternatives to network broadcasting. Communications satellites could carry radio and television messages to every station in the world without using the telephone lines that now link network headquarters to affiliated stations throughout the United States. Indeed, within a decade, and at a manageable cost, satellites will be able to broadcast directly to television sets, bypassing the local stations entirely. Even in the early days of radio broadcasting, it would have been technically possible to broadcast by wire, which would have severely limited the dominance of broadcast stations.

But the then technological limits, as well as the desire of the public to use the receivers they were buying so rapidly—radio was in five million homes by 1926— made "networking" the dominant force in broadcast-

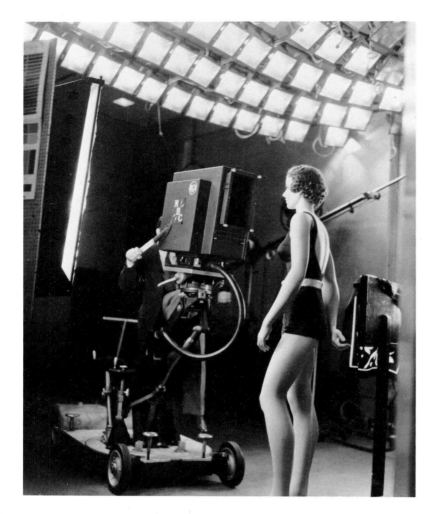

When NBC began experimenting with television from its 30 Rockefeller Plaza headquarters in 1935, they used this model, dubbed "Miss Patience," as a target for the testing of this first-generation iconoscopic camera.

This 1930 photograph shows the entire operation—camera, personality (Felix the Cat on a phonograph turntable) and transmitter (on the table, to the left of the camera)—of W2XBS, which was the forerunner of NBC's New York outlet.

ing. By 1927, the National Broadcasting Company was offering a regular schedule of programs. A year later, NBC came up with the first national programming phenomenon, *Amos 'n' Andy*. Meanwhile, a tiny network of sixteen radio stations called the United Independent Broadcasters was piloted through a series of financial crises by Arthur Judson, George Coats, and Leon Levy of Philadelphia's WCAU. A young cigar company heir, William S. Paley, brought fresh blood—and money—to the network, renamed the Columbia Broadcasting System. By 1929, CBS had overcome its shaky beginnings to stand as a small rival to NBC. (The third major network, the American Broadcasting Company, did not begin until 1943. NBC was operating two different networks—the "red" and the "blue," so named for the colors used for each on the engineers' charts. An FCC ruling in 1941 forced RCA to divest itself of one of the networks. After fighting the case unsuccessfully all the way to the Supreme Court, RCA sold the weaker "blue" network to Edward J. Noble, the Lifesaver king, for $8 million.) And by the time television became a technological reality, the shape of network programming was all but embedded in concrete. It didn't happen without protest. As early as 1933, Senators Robert Wagner of New York and Henry Hatfield of West Virginia proposed the cancellation and redistribution of all radio licenses to counteract commercial domination of the medium. But the move failed; and broadcasting as a medium largely run by private corporations—financed by the dollars of other private corporations through advertising—supplying stations which were operating by virtue of government-supplied monopolies, was a *fait accompli*. Thus, the broadcasting forms of the early twentieth century shaped the form of the most powerful medium of the latter half of that century.

Most people think of television as a post–World War II phenomenon, and indeed that is when its presence was first felt across America. But, as was noted, television was both a promise and a fact even before the twentieth century began. And with the technological breakthroughs of Philo T. Farnsworth and Vladimir Zworykin, television was ready to be launched. Were it not for the Depression and World War II, television almost surely would have been saturating American homes by the end of the 1930s. There were, however, technical problems to be fixed. Because early experiments with the medium involved "low definition" resolution—sometimes as few as 60 lines as opposed to the current 525—there was some doubt as to the full readiness of the medium. In 1933, for example, CBS suspended telecasts because of the poor quality of

NBC's experimental studio, in 1937, and CBS's studios four floors above the tracks in New York's Grand Central Station—shown here in 1939—became the studios from which live television drama began entering American homes on a regular basis a decade later.

RCA's exhibit, the Hall of Television, at the 1939 World's Fair in New York drew huge crowds to witness such marvels of the future as this glass television set. In addition, RCA's broadcasting company, NBC, televised Franklin D. Roosevelt's opening of the fair, making him the first president to appear on television.

reception. But by 1937, Philco demonstrated the first truly high-resolution television picture—using 441 lines. In the same year, the British Broadcasting Corporation began regular television programming. RCA began it in the United States in 1939, and launched it in a manner strikingly reminiscent of the excitement that surrounded the telephone's public debut. Just as Bell had chosen the 1876 Centennial Exposition in Philadelphia to demonstrate his device, RCA chose the 1939 World's Fair for a major promotional effort.

RCA built an exhibit—a Hall of Television, displaying futuristic visions of the medium—and NBC broadcast live from the fairgrounds. President Roosevelt opened the fair, becoming the first American president to appear on television. NBC—which, two years earlier, had a single TV studio in Rockefeller Center producing two programs a week and a mobile unit to cover events outside the studio—portrayed the fair as the beginning of a major surge toward television. But while the medium moved in fits and starts—the 1940 conventions were telecast, and commercial sponsorship began in 1941—the outbreak of World War II brought development to a halt. In 1942, the manufacture of receivers was stopped, and programming was curtailed. Not until 1946 did TV sets go on sale again, and at that time there were ten television stations in the entire country. The coaxial cable, used to transmit television pictures beyond the reach of a signal, linked only the East and did not reach Chicago until 1949.

Before the great television surge began, however, technology once again entered the broadcasting picture, once again in a way that greatly influenced the structure of the medium. There are two ways to send television pictures through the air: on the Very High Frequency band (54 to 216 millions of cycles, or megacycles, per second), and on the Ultra High Frequency band (470 to 890 millions of cycles per second). The technical distinction concerns the number of cycles per second of the waves; the *functional* distinction is that there are far more UHF than VHF channels available. In 1945, the Federal Communications Commission approved thirteen carrier frequencies in the VHF range, designated as Channels 1–13, for television use. (Later Channel 1 was removed from the television band and given over to other uses, such as police and fire calls.) As a practical matter, since some of these channels interfered with adjacent channels, this meant a maximum of seven VHF outlets for even the biggest markets, such as New York or Los Angeles. By contrast, the UHF channels, ranging from 14 to 83, would have provided a potentially wide-ranging set of alternatives

In 1946, the commercial development of television began. The manufacture of receivers, which had been halted in 1942, was resumed, and this RCA assembly line started to turn the product out.

The man who first gave Americans a reason to buy a television set. Here, comedian Milton Berle returns in September, 1949, for a second season as star of *The Texaco Star Theatre*. His Tuesday night show from 8 to 9 P.M. sent East Coast restaurateurs and movie operators into shock; people were staying home to watch Berle's antics.

Some people call television "talking furniture." This 1939 model *(center)* emphasizes its decorative rather than functional aspect. In the promotional photo above, note the symbolism of the radio pushed into a corner of the living room.

for everything from educational television to "elitist" alternatives and community access offerings. Instead, commercial development began on the VHF band. The first UHF station did not begin broadcasting until the fall of 1952, when there were 20 million television sets in use, none of which could receive any UHF stations. (Congress required television set manufacturers to produce only all-channel receivers beginning in 1964, but even then viewers found it difficult to tune in UHF stations because the UHF channels were not divided by recognizable clicks.)

As a consequence, television became technically segregated. The commercial networks, which were viewable almost exclusively on VHF stations, not only attracted 90 percent of the viewing audience on a typical evening (prime time), but viewers would never even pass through the alternative UHF stations on their way around the dial. This "technical" choice—of VHF, because of its stronger signal, over UHF—had consequences that were far greater than a matter of megacycles. Among them was the limiting of actual telecasting to the established broadcasting giants, NBC and CBS. It took ABC until the 1970s to overcome its early weakness in attracting affiliates; and the Du Mont Television Network, unable to build a station lineup, went out of business in 1955.

By the late 1940s, television began its conquest of America. In 1949, the year began with radio drawing 81 percent of all broadcast audiences. By the year's end, television was grabbing 41 percent of the broadcast market. When audiences began experiencing the heady thrill of actually seeing as well as hearing events as they occurred, the superiority of television was established beyond doubt.

By the end of 1950, movie attendance among adults was down 72 percent and radio use had dropped from 3 hours and 42 minutes a night to 24 minutes. Erik Barnouw's definitive history of television, *Tube of Plenty*, recounts these reports of movie theater closings in 1951: eastern Pennsylvania, 70; southern California, 134; Chicago, 64; metropolitan New York City, 55. And the same year, the coaxial cable reached from coast to coast, providing truly nationwide live television. The first *See It Now* program, starring Edward R. Murrow and produced by Murrow and Fred Friendly, featured simultaneous television pictures of the Brooklyn Bridge and the Golden Gate Bridge. This 1951 debut was the symbol of what television had become: a bridge that linked the traditionally heterogenous American nation together as nothing else had ever done.

There remained one major technical development

before television was considered complete—color. There was in the fight over color television a major similarity to the debate about television transmission, again suggesting that economic interest, as well as necessity, is the mother of invention.

As with television itself, color transmission was a fact long before its introduction into general use. As early as 1929, Bell Telephone Laboratories demonstrated color television transmission. All through World War II, RCA and CBS were experimenting with color, and in 1946 CBS colorcast an image from New York City to Nyack, New York, to impress four members of the Federal Communications Commission. CBS expected that the mass marketing of television sets would be delayed until the regulatory commission resolved the broad question of color TV as well. Instead, the FCC held off any decision on color and permitted the marketing of black-and-white sets.

The problem was one of technology and economics. The CBS system used a "color wheel"—a mechanical disk similar in concept to the mechanical scanner developed by Nipkow and refined by Baird and Jenkins in the days before Farnsworth and Zworykin developed the electronic scanner. This color wheel required a spinning disk in the color camera and in the home television set. The black-and-white sets, of course, did not come equipped with any such device. They were, therefore, "incompatible" with the color system. RCA was developing a color system that could also be received in black and white by existing sets. The only problem was that the color quality was terrible.

Had the FCC approved the CBS system in 1947—when fewer than 250,000 existing sets were in use—America might never have passed through the era of black-and-white television. As it delayed the decision, the more black-and-white sets that were sold, the more important it became to develop a system that could be received on those sets. In addition, RCA quickly became the biggest seller of black-and-white sets. Its dominant share of the receiver market made it adamantly opposed to the CBS plan, even though CBS inventor Peter Goldmark developed a converter which could have been linked up to existing black-and-white sets.

Manufacturers of black-and-white sets seized on the point that the CBS color wheel had to be twice the diameter of the picture tube; they argued that such a wheel would, on big-screen sets, pose a clear and present danger. In fact, Du Mont, whose company made black-and-white sets, showed up at an FCC hearing with a six-foot-wide color wheel, suggesting it would likely menace an entire family. In 1950, the FCC gave

The first major news event to transfix the American viewer was the congressional investigation into organized crime chaired by Senator Estes Kefauver (second from left), and spearheaded by committee counsel Rudolph Halley (reading). The hearings made Kefauver into a presidential contender and helped Halley to become president of the New York City Council.

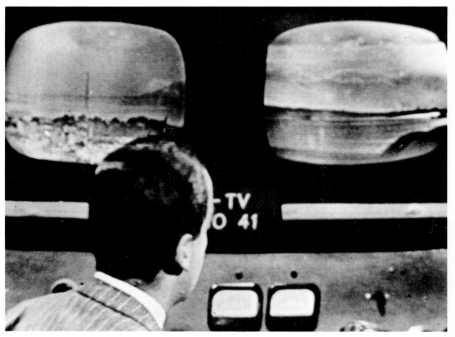

In November, 1951, Edward R. Murrow began a new television program, *See It Now*, by using the new coast-to-coast coaxial cable to telecast pictures of the Brooklyn Bridge and the Golden Gate Bridge at the same time to the same audience. "We are impressed," Murrow said.

Dr. Peter Goldmark of CBS Laboratories shows a 1947 model of a color television set to two rivals, Allen B. Du Mont, president of the Du Mont Corporation (left), and E. W. Engstrom of RCA (center). The two companies, protecting their own production of black-and-white television sets, fought the CBS color system for years, all the way to the Supreme Court.

A first-generation RCA color camera ▶ is used to test compatible color in 1951. Today, a technician can use a battery-operated color "mini-cam," weighing about twenty pounds, to photograph WNBC-TV reporter Bob Teague. This system, and similar "ENG" (electronic news gathering) devices, use half-inch and even quarter-inch video tape, and can transmit signals directly back to a broadcast center without the need for wires or cables of any kind.

To fight the Goldmark "color wheel" television system, Du Mont (left) demonstrated his contention that a large color screen would require a color wheel with a 7-foot diameter and a rim speed of 360 miles per hour. The presentation raised the prospect of dangerous accidents should the huge, rapidly spinning wheel somehow break loose.

CBS founder William S. Paley sits astride an early company color camera in 1951. In June of that year, CBS demonstrated an hour-long color program broadcast to New York, Boston, Philadelphia, Baltimore, and Washington, D.C.

the CBS system its approval, but by the time the Supreme Court upheld the decision in 1951, there were already more than 7.5 million black-and-white sets in use, and the effort to inject a second television receiver into American homes was too complex, too expensive. In 1953, the FCC reversed its decision and went with the RCA all-electronic system, which used three guns to scan for reds, blues, and greens, the primary colors in color television.

In the field of color development, technology once again influenced other aspects of television. For once color became an important part of the American television pattern—and by 1972 there were more color than black-and-white television sets being sold in America—the audience began to demand more and more color programming. The NBC peacock, designed to let audiences know that a program was being broadcast in what was first called "compatible," then "living" color, was born in September, 1957, less than four years after Kukla, Fran, Ollie, and the Boston Pops Orchestra starred on NBC's first "compatible color" broadcast. And NBC in particular, as the one television network with a major interest in the sales of television sets (its parent company, RCA, was one of the largest manufacturers), actively promoted color. This meant that, for example, quality black-and-white movies had an extremely depressed market value for sale to television networks. It meant that the closeup, human conflict dramas in which early TV excelled would be

Meet two-thirds of the first group to be broadcast in compatible color, in 1953, on NBC. Kukla and Fran Allison are here; Oliver J. Dragon is otherwise occupied.

supplanted by the graphic, "big-screen" movie values of color, movement, and action (which is one of the reasons why the face of television drama changed in the late 1950s). In effect, the advent of color gave television a chance to satisfy an audience less by what it said than by the way it said—and showed—it.

A century of technological innovation that brought us the telegraph, the telephone, and the radio—as well as the structural and economic realities originally shaped by these technologies—were combined in the formation of television. Telegraphy had made possible national exchange of news and information on a rapid basis; the telephone not only facilitated personal communication, but created a corporate communications giant whose early influence over radio helped inspire the concept of both network broadcasting and commercial sponsorship of that programming. The growth of genuinely mass media—centered at first in magazines—had given advertisers the potential of marketing a single "brand" product throughout the country, and radio had accelerated that process. Now television would take a single image, a single voice, a single fact—or falsehood—a single mode of speech or dress or style and broadcast it visually, instantaneously, throughout the land. And this medium, by accident more than by design, was in the hands of relatively few people. And, less and less by accident, these people found themselves relatively free from effective control or accountability. This system had grown and taken shape in large measure because the invention had created new categories of reality, new sources of power that the government could not even contemplate until they were firmly in place. By midcentury, television had conquered America. In one sense, we had expected it all along. In another sense, we never knew what hit us.

PRIME TIME

Programming:
Why We See
What We See

Ask a commercial network programmer about improving television and the usual response is that the mass audience "doesn't want Shakespeare and ballet after a hard day's work." It is one reason why such offerings are usually confined to public television. James Earl Jones *(right)* played the lead in *King Lear* from the 1974 *Great Performances* series, and the Merce Cunningham Dance Company *(below)* performed on *Dance in America* in 1977.

When America watches television, it usually watches commercial network television. Public Broadcasting Service—a loosely knit network of about 265 noncommercial stations—offers one alternative. PBS, which supplanted National Educational Television in 1967, is supported by foundation and corporation grants, universities, tax money, and donations from viewers. There are also about 100 local stations which are unaffiliated with a television network; these exist almost exclusively in the biggest cities, with a population large enough to support more than two or three different commercial stations.

But of the roughly seven hundred commercial television stations in the United States, more than six hundred of them are affiliated with one of the three television networks—CBS, NBC, and ABC. While the contracts between networks and local stations do not require the stations to carry network programming—indeed, any such requirement has been specifically outlawed by the Federal Communications Commission—and while local stations do preempt network shows on occasion to carry their own movies, syndicated shows, or locally produced programs, most of what America sees, from early morning to late at night, is programmed by the networks.

The reason is primarily a matter of economics. Theoretically, a local station could make more money by programming its own shows. A network pays its affiliated stations only about 30 percent of the stations' potential advertising revenues to carry its programs and the advertising in those programs (this payment is called station compensation). If a local station produced its own programs, all the revenues from advertising that appeared on those programs would go directly to the station. But no local station could possibly afford to pay the enormous costs of, for example, a one-hour drama (about $300,000) or a half-hour comedy (about $150,000). Nor could any local station afford the $50 million it costs to maintain a typical network news operation for an average year.

The network is not the only supplier of programs. Independent sources of programming have survived, and even flourished, in recent years. Outside of prime time, many network-owned and -affiliated stations use first-run syndicated programs, such as *The Mike Douglas Show*, produced by either a non-network station group (Group W and Metromedia being the two most powerful) or by an independent producer. These shows are shipped to individual stations, who pay a fee based on the size of the station's market. And since 1971, networks have been forbidden by the FCC to supply programs for all of the prime-time hours; under the present application of the Prime-Time Access Rule, they must leave a half hour free six nights a week. In practice, this has turned the half hour after the network news—7:30 P.M. in the East and far West—into a rich source of profits for syndicated game, quiz, variety, and nature shows. Finally, producers who have been rebuffed by the networks have on occasion managed to create hit shows by supplying them on a station-by-station basis. *Space: 1999* and *Mary Hartman, Mary Hartman* are the two most notable products of this system. In the wake of these successes, other television producers are beginning to consider the idea of producing shows without going through networks, and selling them to enough individual stations to make a profit.

For the present, however, the network provides by far the simplest structure for financing high-budget programming. When a station carries a network show, it merely pushes a button, inserts its own commercials during the "word from our local station" break (keeping all of the revenues from its local ads), and clears a profit with minimum effort. Industry figures suggest that VHF station owners earn an average return of more than *30 percent a year* on their original investment. With this kind of all-but-guaranteed profit, the incentive to develop an alternative to network programming is negligible.

While networks program throughout the day, evening, and night, the most visible and prestigious programming is from 7 P.M. until 11 P.M. Eastern time—prime-time programming. This is prime time because most people watch television during those hours. Between 8 P.M. and 9 P.M. on an average weekday night during the fall and winter, two-thirds of all American households with a television—and that means two-thirds of about 97 percent of American homes—are

The top-rated *Gunsmoke*, which began on CBS in 1955, was saved from cancellation in 1967 after CBS chief William Paley personally restored it to the schedule; programming aides had argued that it was reaching the "wrong" audience—too old, too rural. It lasted until 1975.

tuned into something on television. And roughly 90 percent of this audience is watching a program supplied by one of the three commercial networks. Since most people watch television during prime time, this is when the battle for the advertising dollar is most intense. In 1975, I asked an NBC vice-president why the networks were so nervous about prime-time ratings, when they made money even without winning the "race" for the biggest audience.

"It isn't very complicated," he said patiently. "Last year [the September, 1974–April, 1975 season] CBS beat us by *one rating point*. That meant a difference of about seventeen million dollars, eighty-five percent of which was pure profit: because it costs just about as much to put on a show that's a flop as it does a show that's a hit."

To wage this battle, networks examine program possibilities from different sources: from Los Angeles–based production companies, such as Universal, Paramount, Twentieth Century-Fox, Warner Brothers, MGM, and other movie companies; from independent producers who have built their own companies, such as Mary Tyler Moore's MTM Productions and Norman Lear, to take two well-known examples; from inside their own companies. However, for reasons of both economy and fear of antitrust proceedings, networks produce relatively few prime-time shows. By

contrast, the networks have an all-but-inflexible rule *against* any outside news documentaries, ostensibly because they must bear full responsibility for mistakes in news judgment.

The process of selecting shows for a network prime-time schedule is, to an outsider, Byzantine. A constant process of meetings, meals, telephone calls, and tentative deals between network executives, producers, writers, and performers weeds out program ideas from a pool of literally thousands. The selected ideas are continually reviewed, and most are discarded, as they go through the process of development: from an outline, called a treatment, to a script to a pilot show. Then marathon scheduling sessions are held during which the executives at each network attempt to decide which of their old and new shows will best draw and hold an audience away from the offerings of a competing network.

The most common misconception most people have about television concerns its product. To the viewer, the product is the programming. To the television executive, the product is the *audience*.

Strictly speaking, television networks and stations do not make any money by producing a program that audiences want to watch. The money comes from selling advertisers the right to broadcast a message to that audience. The programs exist to capture the

The Lawrence Welk Show (left) was wiped off the ABC schedule for demographic reasons in 1971; CBS did the same to Hee Haw (bottom) and The Beverly Hillbillies (below). Hee Haw and The Lawrence Welk Show have flourished since in first-run syndication, while The Beverly Hillbillies is seen around the country in syndicated reruns.

biggest possible audiences. And the more people who watch a program, the higher the rate that can be charged for advertising time, especially when that audience has the right "demographics"—i.e., when it has a high percentage of economically desirable viewers, generally meaning eighteen- to forty-nine-year-old members of the middle and upper classes.

Once this elementary fact is understood, many of the programming decisions made over the course of television's history become clear.

• Documentaries have all but disappeared from commercial prime-time television, because documentaries tend to drive viewers away from a network. Once driven away, viewers may remain away for an entire evening, and perhaps establish new viewing patterns. A network might well accept the loss of several million viewers for an hour; by its standards—to produce the highest possible profit for the parent corporation and the stockholders—it cannot accept the risk of losing that audience for an entire evening, much less an entire season.

• Throughout television history, popular shows have been canceled not just because the ratings have been low, but because the audience has not been sufficiently attractive economically. In 1967, Gunsmoke

was saved from cancellation only through the personal intervention of CBS founder and chairman of the board, William S. Paley. Despite the program's high ratings, its audience was deemed too old, too rural. Even when the long-running western was canceled in 1975, it was still one of the thirty most popular shows in America. Other shows that were canceled despite high ratings because they drew primarily older or rural viewers include ABC's The Lawrence Welk Show and

First shown on CBS in early 1971 after ABC rejected the Norman Lear pilot, the excellence of All in the Family's cast (right; from right, Jean Stapleton, Carroll O'Connor, Sally Struthers, and Rob Reiner) and its unusual frankness in political and sexual matters made it the country's most popular show. From All in the Family came Maude (below; played by Beatrice Arthur, shown here with Bill Macy as her husband, Walter, and Hermione Baddeley as the new maid), who made her first appearance as Edith's liberal cousin. Maude, in turn, begat Good Times (below, center), starring Esther Rolle, center (as Florida Evans, formerly Maude's maid), with John Amos (as her now-deceased husband), and BernNadette Stanis (as their daughter Thelma). All in the Family also bred The Jeffersons (bottom), starring Sherman Hemsley as George and Isabel Sanford as Louise. Marla Gibbs, left, plays their maid.

CBS's Hee Haw. A raft of rural-based CBS comedies (The Beverly Hillbillies, Petticoat Junction, Green Acres, Mayberry R.F.D.) were all wiped off the schedule in the early 1970s for fear that they were alienating more sophisticated urban and suburban audiences.

• Whether in variety, situation comedy, drama, or the informal talk shows, the primary quest of the networks and stations is for an appealing personality or character. Indeed, this proves to be increasingly true in sports and news as well; audiences become involved with the personal side of athletes, and choose among the warmest, most likable news readers who are, after all, presenting the same substantive information. This concern for character and personality is evident throughout television's history: in the longevity of such

The Mary Tyler Moore Show, which debuted in 1970, was an uncommonly funny and sensitive portrayal of a modern career woman and her worker-friends. It retired as an undefeated champion in 1977, but the two shows it spawned are still running. Rhoda Morgenstern (top; with Ted Baxter, played by Ted Knight, and Mary Tyler Moore) went off to New York and an uncertain future in Rhoda. Valerie Harper's characterization of a smart, attractive, neurotic Jewish girl was fine, but the show floundered trying to balance Rhoda's independence against her marriage. Cloris Leachman (above) as Phyllis, whose show began in 1975, faced a different problem: how do you make a character who was essentially unpleasant appealing as a lead? Making her a widow was not enough; the show was canceled after two seasons.

low-key, informal personalities as Dinah Shore, Johnny Carson, Ed Sullivan, Garry Moore, and Mike Douglas; in the consistent emphasis on warm, familial bonds even in such situation comedies with "bite" as All in the Family and Maude; in the movement of television drama away from anthology shows and toward regular dramatic series involving an attractive personality threatened by danger week after week.

• The concern for character also accounts for the "spin-off"—a series built around a popular secondary character from another series. When All in the Family became the most popular show in America, CBS took the character of Archie Bunker's acerbic cousin, Maude Finley, and featured her in her own series. The success of that show led to the spinning-off of

The Bob Newhart Show (*left*; he's shown here with Marcia Wallace portraying girl-Friday Carol), produced and written by the same company that did *The Mary Tyler Moore Show*, MTM Productions, had an ambience similar to *The Mary Tyler Moore Show*. More important, it had *MTM* as a lead-in, as CBS sought to preserve the all-important "audience flow." ABC did the same with *Laverne & Shirley* (*right*; starring Cindy Williams and Penny Marshall). The characters were drawn from the top-rated *Happy Days*; the show was scheduled right after *Happy Days*; and the youth-cult Fonzie character appeared in the first few shows. Result? A smash hit.

Maude's maid, Florida, into her own series, *Good Times*. The Bunkers' next-door neighbors, an upwardly mobile black family, the Jeffersons, were also given their own series. *The Mary Tyler Moore Show* followed this same pattern; two supporting characters each wound up in their own shows, *Rhoda* and *Phyllis*.

The reason for this practice, which dates back at least as far as *Mayberry R.F.D.*, the offspring of *The Andy Griffith Show*, is that these supporting characters have already built audience loyalty. No network programmer, no producer, no star, however smart or successful, can know in advance whether a character is going to win the hearts and minds of the mass audience. A character who has proven his or her appeal is several steps ahead of the game.

• A typical prime-time network schedule is deliberately designed so as *not* to produce radical shifts in audience. Networks do not want audiences moving to switch the dial. As one successful television producer has put it, "We're a medicine show. We're here to deliver the audience to the next commercial. So the basic network policy is to set in motion from the beginning of prime time to the end of prime time, programs to maintain and deliver those audiences to the commercial."

Since, in the famous dictum of NBC programming executive Paul Klein, people do not turn on television to watch programs but to watch *television*, programs are designed as "building blocks" to maintain "audience flow." If *The Mary Tyler Moore Show* is a hit, follow

it with *The Bob Newhart Show* from the same production company, which has the same general ambience, and you keep the huge audience delivered by Mary Tyler Moore. If *Happy Days* becomes a huge audience magnet for ABC, make the next half hour *Laverne & Shirley*, again developed by the same production company. The half-hour triumph becomes an hour triumph, and the advertising rates are kept high.

The men and women (still almost exclusively men) who program for prime-time America do not argue that the programs they choose for their schedules meet their personal tastes. As a former network vice-president said, "It's not what I personally like that matters. What you ask is, 'Will thirty million Americans watch this?' I'm not programming for my friends or your friends. I'm programming for people—people who are less educated than I am, who travel less, who read fewer books."

They argue, rather, that this is what people *want* to watch (former NBC president Reuven Frank calls this the "drug pusher's argument"). And the steady increase in the time they spend watching television, which now keeps American televisions on for an average of almost seven hours a day, buttresses that claim.

But there is an equally powerful counterargument. No one knows whether an audience will accept a new kind of programming until it is tried. It was once a given that sixty minutes was the maximum length for a prime-time television program. The made-for-TV movies and the long-form shows such as *The Virginian* disproved that maxim. It was another maxim that a network should not disrupt its regular schedule to pre-

The made-for-TV movie, such as NBC's *Sybil* (*above*; starring Sally Field and Joanne Woodward), helped prove that television audiences would tolerate "long-form" dramas, ninety minutes or two hours in length, provided the story lines and characters were strong enough. In 1977, ABC presented *Roots*, the story of a black American's ancestry, on eight consecutive nights. *Roots* (*overleaf*) became the most widely watched show in the history of American television, and helped network executives rethink their conceptions of what kinds of programming would capture a mass audience. Here, the young Kunta Kinte (played by LeVar Burton, *center*), captured by slave traders, awaits the long voyage to America.

sent an excessive number of specials. But, to take two more recent examples, ABC cleared its winter and summer schedules in 1976 for the Olympics and won huge audiences; and part of the record-breaking audience for ABC's *Roots* was due to its scheduling on eight consecutive nights in January, 1977.

Rules and trends are never handed down from a mountaintop, carved in stone. They are invented, rather, to explain an audience hunger that frequently is aroused by the taste of something new, a hunger that cannot be sated by the taste of something familiar. A look at the three staples of prime-time programming—variety, situation comedy, and drama—will suggest how the demands of network programming helped and hindered the development of new forms, of attempts to break the mold of conformity. It will show how television in its early days, as a new medium without rules, was indeed more adventurous and diverse than when it became established and dependent on network formulas. And it will also reveal where the seeds of potential change—sometimes produced by the same competitive pressures—are now budding.

There is one more point to keep in mind. It is often said that television programming is produced out of fear—a fear of failing to earn enough profits to satisfy corporate boards of directors, fear of offending any of the innumerable special interest groups that keep watch over television. Certainly there is enough in television's past—from the acquiescence in the political blacklist of talent to the persistent limits on the themes of television drama and the enormous distance between emotional reality and the emotions of television characters—to warrant that conclusion.

But television does not exist in a vacuum. It exists in a system of competitive risks and rewards that, in the case of the television industry, has served to minimize those risks and maximize those rewards. It is by now an industry that takes in almost $6 billion in revenues yearly. In 1976, according to the Federal Communications Commission, the three television networks and the fifteen stations they own took in $2.6 billion in revenues; they made a combined pretax profit of $454 million, an increase of 44.5 percent in a single year.

What these figures mean is that, for all of the rhetoric about television serving as a "window on the world" or an arm of the "public interest," television is big business. And Norman Lear, one of television's most successful producers and a man who has pushed the limits of the medium outward, has said:

Television is another industry in America. It gets enormous attention because of its visibility. But it's run like all of those other industries. . . . If the major oil companies did well selling you an additive last year, they're going to find another additive plus this year, and they're going to raise prices again. They're going to do what they can within the economic system to improve their profits, and to continue giving the public what it seemed to want last year.

As long as television is structurally schizophrenic—that is, as long as licenses are given to stations to serve a "public interest" that station owners equate with programming for maximum profit by the constant appeal to mass audiences—Lear's view will remain accurate. For these profits mean affluence for the television community—including the writers, producers, actors, and directors who criticize it—which is the most powerful incentive imaginable to keep things as they are. So those with the best chance to do something different are those who know best how to keep things the same.

Variety:
From the
Sensational
to the
Conversational —
and
Back Again

The first promise of television was elemental: for the first time, in the comfort and privacy of their living rooms, people could see what was happening, as it was happening, right before their eyes. The sheer presence of pictures, of talent, of movement was enough in the early days of television to hypnotize an audience. And thus, the first major successes on television—apart from borrowed forms such as wrestling matches and old Hopalong Cassidy movies—were variety shows. In 1948, three of the most important early television shows made their debuts: *The Texaco Star Theatre*, with Milton Berle; *Arthur Godfrey's Talent Scouts*; and *Toast of the Town*, with Ed Sullivan. A year later, Sid Caesar and Imogene Coca came on the air with *The Admiral Broadway Revue,* later changed to *Your Show of Shows*.

Yet these four shows sharply diverged in their approach and format, creating a number of distinct patterns in variety shows that run through the development of the medium. In particular, the Berle and Sullivan shows relied heavily on excitement, on a sense of show business pace that is traceable to the days of vaudeville and the fast-moving, gala Broadway revues. Arthur Godfrey, in his personality and in the format of his shows, represented the relaxed, informal, "homey" approach, which used the television set less as a bridge into a glamorous world of show business and more as a harmonious part of the living room itself. This approach has subsequently flourished from daytime to late night.

Consider *The Texaco Star Theatre*. An orchestra plays an up-tempo tune as a quartet of gas-station attendants sing the opening theme. They introduce, to drumrolls, the star, Milton Berle. He appears suddenly, dressed in an outlandish costume—perhaps as the Easter Bunny or a giant valentine heart; often he was in women's clothing. He strides around the stage, mugging, leering, his face a rubber mask of contortions. He introduces the first act: jugglers, acrobats, or perhaps an animal act. Something for the eye; something you can see. The jokes are right out of burlesque: the seltzer squirt, the pie in the face, the cry of "*Maaaake*up!" followed by a makeup puff right in Berle's face.

Consider the Sullivan show, the acts following one another in dizzy succession: jugglers, acrobats, dan-

The outrageous comedy of Milton Berle on *The Texaco Star Theatre* in 1948 was the first major success on commercial television. In this NBC Tuesday night show, Berle paraded across the stage in outlandish dress, often donning women's clothes, as in this parody *(opposite page)* of Carmen Miranda (a frequent guest on the Berle show). He made himself the butt of the show's humor, with wisecracking assistants (such as Arnold Stang; *left*) who put down the king of comedy. Berle merged his talent with another early television success, *Howdy Doody* (*bottom*; Buffalo Bob Smith, center, and the childlike Clarabell, right, are shown here along with Berle as cutup kid). Comedian Martha Raye and singer-dancer Ray Bolger *(below, left)* join Berle in one of the later shows before the Berle phenomenon burned itself out.

New York *Daily News* gossip columnist Ed Sullivan hosted *Toast of the Town* in 1948. Its first show *(opposite page, top row, center)* starred, among others, the new comedy team of Dean Martin and Jerry Lewis. Although Sullivan completely lacked any gift for entertaining, his Sunday night show brought a wide range of talent to television. A devoted participant in television's political blacklisting of the early 1950s, Sullivan was also committed to presenting black talent, such as Louis Armstrong *(middle row, left)* and Pearl Bailey *(middle row, right)*. He also brought all manner of celebrities to his show, both on stage *(bottom row, left;* as in this show with members of the 1951 New York Yankees, the World Series champions), and by introducing them from the audience. "High-class talent" *(top row, left;* in this 1951 ensemble, Richard Rodgers, Oscar Hammerstein II, and Gertrude Lawrence offer songs from *The King and I)* was a regular feature of *The Ed Sullivan Show*, as was new Hollywood talent; here *(top row, right)* he talks with Ann-Margret.

Sullivan's two most remembered acts were from different generations of rock 'n' roll. Elvis Presley *(middle row, center)*, who appeared three times on Sullivan's show in the mid-1950s, so shocked segments of the audience with a particularly pelvic rendition of "Hound Dog" that in his next appearance he was photographed only from the waist up. And in 1964, Sullivan featured the Beatles *(bottom row, right)*, probably the most popular rock act of all time.

Your Show of Shows began on NBC in 1950 on Saturday nights. Although it presented a variety of singers, dancers, and comedians, the show's centerpiece was the comedy team of Sid Caesar and Imogene Coca *(top)*. They were backed by the talents of second bananas Carl Reiner *(above; right)* and Howard Morris, and a writing stable with some of the funniest television writers the medium ever employed, including Mel Brooks, Neil Simon, and Larry Gelbart.

cers, animal acts ("I was booked on the Sullivan show," Don Rickles once cracked, "but my bear died"). His show featured masses of people: the West Point Glee Club, the New York City Ballet. He turned live cameras on a fireworks display in the New York City harbor ("Let's really hear it for the fireworks!" he implored his audience).

Even the Caesar show, remembered for the brilliant comic talents of Caesar, Coca, Carl Reiner, and Howard Morris, and a writing team that included Neil Simon and Mel Brooks, featured the Billy Williams Quartet, Marguerite Piazza, the Bob Hamilton Trio, and dancers Bambi Linn and Rod Alexander, both to break the pace of the skits and to provide visual entertainment.

Arthur Godfrey was a different kind of performer. His appeal, both on the *Talent Scouts* show and on *Arthur Godfrey and His Friends*, depended less on excitement and more on the public warmth and accessibility of Godfrey himself. His show was an offering of familial affection. Announcer Tony Marvin, singers Frank Parker and Marion Marlowe (were they really in love?), the McGuire Sisters, Haleloke, singer Julius LaRosa, and bandleader Archie Bleyer were not just professionals. Godfrey talked to them, let the viewers know them as people. The reality of conflict, the on-the-air firing of LaRosa, did not matter. For Godfrey had provided a method of reaching the television audience that was particularly well-suited to the medium. He had an instinctive understanding that this living-room furniture, intimately present in the homes of viewers, could be made an enormously powerful substitute for real familial bonds.

These first variety shows, then, displayed three distinct forms: first, the host as talent (Caesar and Berle), blending his or her skills into a broadly appealing show. Second, the host as broker of talent (Sullivan), offering a blend of comedy, song, dance, and spectacle. Third, the host as friend (Godfrey), subordinating talent to the fact of his presence. What is curious—and revealing—is that the medium tended to provide far more longevity to the last two categories than to the first.

Milton Berle, the first giant star of television, the man who closed down restaurants and movie theaters at eight o'clock on Tuesday nights, was soundly beaten in the ratings by Phil Silvers's army situation comedy, *You'll Never Get Rich*, and taken off the air in 1956, long since deposed as ratings king. Sid Caesar was conquered by Lawrence Welk in 1957, but he had lost his Saturday night spot by 1954. These outsized talents were burned out by television; it was almost as if

A low-key, low-pressure, informal radio star named Arthur Godfrey made an easy transition to television in the late 1940s. For years he had two weekly prime-time shows, *Arthur Godfrey's Talent Scouts*, and *Arthur Godfrey and His Friends* (Godfrey is shown here, with Dr. Frank Stanton, then president of CBS, center, and Hawaiian singer Haleloke, far right). Note the studied informality of the set, as if he and his friends were having an evening of fun in his living room.

Red Skelton, shown here as Freddie the Freeloader, one of his enduring characters, was a mainstay of the CBS prime-time schedule for more than a decade.

Jack Benny (shown here with Irish tenor Dennis Day) so carefully cultivated his image on radio that the transition to television was easy. His variety show was actually a situation comedy about a stingy comedian named Jack Benny, and the misadventures he and his colleagues had in putting on a television show.

they could not survive the expending of so much sheer energy. By contrast, Ed Sullivan remained on the air for twenty-three years.

This is not to say that talent does not survive on television in the variety format. Red Skelton lasted on CBS for nearly twenty years; Jack Benny had a run on CBS television that lasted fifteen years; Carol Burnett has been on CBS for a decade; and Bob Hope was an NBC drawing card for more than twenty years. Talent, however, is not enough. Television seems to demand from its variety principals a particular kind of personality: low-key, easygoing, friendly, amiable. A warm personality can survive without talent. So can a personality audiences come to know and trust, even without the warmth; Ed Sullivan is a prime example. Talent without that personality cannot succeed.

Some of radio's most popular personalities could not make the transition successfully into television. The zany Ed Wynn, the acerbic Fred Allen were two early examples. Singers who were enormously gifted, compelling in person and on records, tried and failed at regular television variety shows—Frank Sinatra and

Two of the long-distance runners of television, Bob Hope and Jack Benny, here join forces. CBS's "capture" of Benny from NBC in the late 1940s gave that network its first success against NBC as a prime-time ratings champion. Hope has been a mainstay of NBC—with both regular shows and specials—since the earliest days of television.

One of the most successful variety shows of the late 1950s starred Garry Moore (*top*; left), an amiable performer of no particular talent. His announcer, sidekick, and commercial spokesman, Durwood Kirby, was of similar dimensions. But a female second banana, Carol Burnett, went on to host what is now the longest running and most successful prime-time variety show on the air. She's shown *(above)* with long-time regular, Harvey Korman.

Fred Allen was one of the giants of radio comedy, with an acerbic wit and a deliberate posture of "anti-friendliness." He did not, however, do well on television; after this 1953 attempt, he was generally confined to panel shows.

"Lonesome George Gobel" was a Saturday night star in the late 1950s, popularizing homey expressions ("Well, I'll be a dirty bird"). Along with many variety hosts, Gobel built a situation-comedy sketch into the variety format.

Judy Garland, shown here in 1956 on a *General Electric Theatre* special, was one of many supremely talented performers who could not sustain a weekly television show.

Judy Garland are two prime examples. Those that made the transition had something more to commend them to television audiences. Among radio personalities, Jack Benny had built such a strong *persona*, such a family of supporting characters, that he was in fact part of a situation comedy in the guise of a variety show. (Many long-running variety shows presented situation comedies as part of the variety show, most notably Jackie Gleason with "The Honeymooners," which later became a half-hour comedy. Carol Burnett today has one of the most brutally funny "mini-sit-coms," with her "Family.") Among singers who made the switch, Dinah Shore and Perry Como, both with easygoing charm, have survived for years as successful television performers.

As television moved west, as the filmed series became the dominant TV mode, as syndication of film became the surest route to big money, the appeal of the live variety show faded for producers. With their use of topical jokes and contemporary songs and guest stars, they proved impossible to syndicate for

Dinah Shore, who succeeded in both prime time and daytime, combined singing talent, a "perky" personality, and a big goodnight kiss to win her audiences. Louis Prima and Keely Smith, George Montgomery and Dinah, Ernie Kovacs and Edie Adams—all married couples at the time—came together here.

Jackie Gleason as Ralph Kramden, bus driver, and Art Carney as Ed Norton, sewer worker, share a moment of intellectual curiosity in Kramden's apartment in *The Honeymooners*. In reruns today, *The Honeymooners* still comes across as one of the funniest situation comedies.

His relaxed mood sparked many jokes ("Did you see Perry Como?" "No, I fell asleep." "So did he"), but Perry Como starred in a high-rated NBC variety show. He still draws audiences to his specials.

Despite their amiable manner, the Smothers Brothers, in the late 1960s, starred in one of the few hit variety shows to stand in direct opposition to mainstream values. Tom and Dick are shown here with two well-known television couples, Barbara Bain and Martin Landau (then from *Mission: Impossible*), and Sonny and Cher.

One of the more inventive variety shows in its use of television was Flip Wilson's NBC Thursday night show of the early 1970s.

reruns once their network runs were over. This meant that the biggest source of windfall profits was foreclosed to variety performers and producers. At the same time, as television became a familiar presence in the American living room, the original premise of the variety format became untenable; it was no longer enough simply to show the viewers that something was happening in front of their eyes. Those variety shows that succeeded in prime time had to offer something special. In the late 1960s, the Smothers Brothers beat the once invincible western, *Bonanza*, by being the first explicitly antiwar, antiestablishment television show. In their comedy skits, in their choice of guests (Pete Seeger, Joan Baez), in their public battles with the CBS network, the Smothers Brothers were unique: an act with mass public appeal that was in opposition to mainstream values. Their public disputes proved too much for the network, which canceled the show in the spring of 1969.

Flip Wilson achieved success as a variety show host—the first black to do so—with a format that was

clearly adjusted to the world of television. Most variety shows worked off a proscenium stage, with the television camera in effect occupying "the best seat in the house." Wilson's show was mounted as theater-in-the-round, with the audience surrounding the stage, and used light, mobile sets and a minimum of props. In this sense, the show acknowledged Bertolt Brecht's principle of alienation; the audience was always aware that it was watching a television show. As the skits ended, the camera would pull back to show the movement of sets and actors.

Probably no show used the medium of television more aggressively than *Rowan and Martin's Laugh-In* on NBC. From the time it began in January, 1968, it captivated the audience, especially the younger viewers who had grown up with television. While the show's popularity was relatively short-lived—it was canceled in 1973—the use of black-outs, fast-paced cutting, and constant flash-backs and flash-forwards was innovative. Although it owed a debt to television's original mad genius, Ernie Kovacs, it was much more ex-

From 1950 in Philadelphia, through four television networks, until his death in 1962 while creating monthly specials for ABC—no one was more creative, no one pushed the comic possibilities of television further than did Ernie Kovacs. He created a raft of characters (Bavarian Disk Jockey Wolfgang Sauerbraten is one of them), parodied old television shows, and played visual tricks on his audiences through such devices as chromakeying (rendering people and objects invisible) and mixing images.

Rowan and Martin's Laugh-In borrowed liberally from such diverse sources as burlesque, vaudeville, and early television creators like Steve Allen and Ernie Kovacs. The fast-paced, often freewheeling one-hour show was aimed at an audience used to the quick cuts and instant transitions of television. Everyone from John Wayne to Richard Nixon cooperated in filming cameo shots, and Dinah Shore *(far left)* stepped miles out of character for this 1971 guest appearance. *Laugh-In* also provided the first showcase for Tiny Tim *(left;* center) and "Tiptoe Through the Tulips."

Late-night television began in earnest with NBC's *Broadway Open House (left)*, featuring the antics of knockabout comic Jerry Lester. He is shown here with accordionist Milton de Lugg and Dagmar, whose appeal Lester exploited ceaselessly. Steve Allen *(right)* later took over the show, (renamed *The Tonight Show*),and presided over a low-key, informal collection of singers (Steve Lawrence and Eydie Gormé), comics, and offbeat personalities such as Ben Belafont, the rhyming inventor.

Watching Jack Paar, who hosted *The Tonight Show* from 1957 until 1962, was like watching a tipsy aerialist working without a net. He was nervous, contentious, self-obsessed—and it often led to compelling television. Paar, shown *(right)* with singer Geneviève and Cliff Arquette as Charlie Weaver, walked off his show once in 1960 to protest censorship.

perimental than the conventional variety show. *Laugh-In* was also politically and sexually open; hosts Dan Rowan and Dick Martin gibed at politicians without irritating the network the way the Smothers Brothers alienated the executives at CBS. (Despite the liberal tone of the show, the politician who benefited most from *Laugh-In* was Richard Nixon, who as the 1968 Republican presidential nominee appeared in a

black-out sequence asking "Sock it to *me*?" in an attempt to prove he was able to laugh at himself.)

While the variety format was struggling to regain a place in prime time—at one point in 1975 there were only two prime-time variety shows on the three networks combined—it became securely ensconced all across the rest of the television day by applying the fundamental premise that Godfrey had brought to

For fifteen years, late-night television in America has meant *The Tonight Show* with Johnny Carson, a comedian with a naughty-boy quality and a capacity to reinforce the audience's expectations with almost ritualistic repetition. The jokes that Carnac the Magnificent tells are supposed to be bad; announcer Ed McMahon *(left)* is supposed to be a tippler; "Stump the Band" is a vehicle for Carson to mingle with the audience, and the jokes about the monologue are as important as the monologue itself.

television—the premise of informality.

The Tonight Show, which first began as Jerry Lester's *Broadway Open House*, was launched in 1954 as a part of NBC president Sylvester "Pat" Weaver's notion of a magazine-format show to occupy early morning, midday, and late-night television. (He succeeded at all but the midday idea, where Arlene Francis's *Home* lasted four seasons.) Under a succession of

hosts, from Steve Allen to Jack Paar to Johnny Carson (with a disastrous interlude when Jack Lescoulie was host), the show became progressively more formal, in the sense that there were locked-in nightly rituals. Allen was always good for a fling into the audience or a spontaneous burst of offbeat humor. Jack Paar was sufficiently moody to launch a feud, as he did with columnists Walter Winchell and Dorothy Kilgallen. But

The success of Carson has inspired many similar shows, with varying degrees of success. *The Merv Griffin Show (top)* worked well in syndication but failed as a CBS alternative to Carson (Griffin used Arthur Treacher as his Ed McMahon). Mike Douglas *(second from top)* has been on the air for more than fifteen years (he's shown here with Ella Fitzgerald, Gene Kelly, and Fred Astaire). Joey Bishop *(third from top)*, here with announcer Regis Philbin, was the star of ABC's unsuccessful attempt to compete for the *Tonight Show* audience. Dick Cavett *(above)* offered a more thoughtful mix of talk than did Carson—he's shown here with Norman Mailer—but the late-night audience preferred Carson's polish.

Johnny Carson has succeeded for fifteen years not just because of a superb sense of comic timing, but by providing his late-night audience with a comfortable, reassuring presence. They know he will mock his monologue; they know that his sidekick, Ed McMahon, will laugh excessively; they know Carson will make fun of Doc Severinsen's wardrobe, McMahon's drinking, Burbank's senior citizens.

The look, the set, the feel of *The Tonight Show* and of syndicated talk-variety shows with such popular hosts as Merv Griffin, Mike Douglas, and Dinah Shore negate the original premise of "show business." They do not glitter; they are not glamorous; they are not even very exciting. They are designed to make the audience feel that the show is a part of their neighborhood, part of their home environment, where interesting people come and talk about the daily events of their lives: flying up to Vegas, working on a film, a humorous adventure on vacation. These shows act, in fact, as surrogate salons, providing a sense of communal exchange to people who live increasingly atomized lives. The talk ought not be *too* pretentious or serious, as Dick Cavett learned. But these shows have succeeded because they have not sought to follow the old-fashioned Broadway show business tradition of "knocking the audiences out." Most television audiences don't *want* to be "knocked out." They want, instead, to be included in.

In recent years, an alternate current has begun to stir in variety programming. Some shows have sought to recapture the excitement and glamour of television's early days by exploiting the medium's visual appeal in a contemporary way—the color, the glitter, the lights, the costumes. The original *Sonny and Cher Comedy Hour*, which began in 1971, was the first effort in this direction. Cher's costumes were spectacular. The cameras caught the action from unique angles, often shooting directly out at the audience from behind the performers, capturing not only the cheering audience but the glint of spotlights. The acts were broken up by short bursts of animated tomfoolery—a debt to *Laugh-In*. The orchestrations were brassy and full.

The premise was that audiences could be awakened by the show business values that most variety shows, and in particular the informal, talk-show brand of variety show, had dispensed with. This premise was probably illustrated most spectacularly in the special that Cher Bono did as a solo show in 1975.

The return of show business glitter to variety shows was ▶ nowhere better illustrated than in this Cher special *(following two pages)* in 1975, starring Bette Midler, Elton John, and Flip Wilson. The lavish costumes, sets, and imaginative use of color signified a return to the original concept of television variety—visual dazzle.

Featuring Bette Midler, Elton John, and Flip Wilson, the special was an incredibly lavish display of satin, glitter, wild sets, and surrealistic effects.

The same principle was applied to the ABC variety show *Donny & Marie*, which began in January, 1976. The two principals, members of the highly successful Osmond family, are in one sense pure carbon copies of Sonny and Cher (although it must be a source of comfort to ABC executives that they cannot get divorced). They bicker with each other, insult one another, and have virtually no comic talent whatsoever. They are, however, enveloped in special effects. They are costumed in full color; the show begins each week with an ice-skating number. One regular feature of the show finds Donny and Marie singing with two different groups of back-up singers and two different orchestras.

This suggests that the variety format has come full circle. From a fascination with the purely visual attraction of television, the medium found that it could guarantee success most easily with a personality and a format that did not overwhelm the audience but blended in with it. More recently, an attempt has begun to wake the audience up; to remind it with color, sets, and costumes that television can still catch the eye of an increasingly jaded viewing audience.

An eighteen-year-old boy and a sixteen-year-old girl hosting their own television show? *Donny & Marie*, of the slickly polished Osmond family, debuted in 1976, surrounded by costumes, elaborate sets, and an ice follies feature.

The Brady Bunch, a situation comedy series from 1969 to 1974, was resuscitated by ABC as a variety special. It, too, relied heavily on elaborate visual props.

Studs Terkel came from Chicago. He was blacklisted from television because of his political views, but later gained renown as the author of *Working* and *Hard Times*. Here he hosts an early show, *Studs' Place*.

Many pioneers of "low-pressure" television variety came out of Chicago. Dave Garroway was the first to move in a direction alien to the New York-Broadway-nightclub style. Apart from his *Today* show work, he was host of *Garroway at Large*, originating from this crowded Chicago studio (shown in 1951).

Indiana-born Herb Shriner, a rural anecdotalist, turned that image into a television career, hosting quiz and variety shows. He's shown here on *The Herb Shriner Show* with an unlikely companion, Orson Welles.

Bishop Fulton J. Sheen was television's first religious "star"; his show, *Life Is Worth Living*, ran on ABC, where he appeared opposite Milton Berle.

A precursor of the celebrity talk show, enabling viewers to feel a sense of intimacy with the famous, was *The Stork Club,* ostensibly originating from Sherman Billingsley's famous New York night spot. In this 1950 show, Billingsley (right) talks with Kay Thompson, Ethel Merman, and an unidentified man.

He couldn't sing, dance, or tell a joke, but Art Linkletter had an affable way about him which audiences liked. He hosted game shows *(People Are Funny)*, as well as a series of daytime variety shows, most notably *Art Linkletter's House Party* on CBS. This is a shot from *The Art Linkletter Show,* which ran on NBC in 1963.

NBC executive Sylvester "Pat" Weaver's midafternoon magazine-format show, *Home,* with Arlene Francis, lasted only a few years.

From 1969 to 1972, British personality David Frost hosted a syndicated nightly show, which pioneered the idea of interviewing a single guest—here, Shirley MacLaine. In 1977, Frost won headlines by interviewing—and paying $600,000 for the privilege—former president Richard Nixon.

Faye Emerson had her own show in the first days of television. Her décolletage once caused a national uproar. She poses here with the musical headliner of her show, Skitch Henderson.

Kay Kyser, the dean of the "Kollege of Musical Knowledge" did not last long on television, but his guest selection was certainly eclectic.

One of the charms of *The Arthur Murray Party* can be seen here: the mix of Kathryn Murray's ebullience with Arthur's stony countenance.

Dorothy Collins and Johnny Desmond were two stars of a long-running radio and television show, *Your Hit Parade*, sponsored by Lucky Strike cigarettes. The show died in 1958, a victim of changing musical tastes.

NBC was the first to use a black performer as host of a variety show, *The Nat King Cole Show*, in 1956. Many Southern affiliates refused to carry it, and it failed.

Sing Along with Mitch was a popular NBC show in the early 1960s. The girl just under Miller's left arm is Leslie Uggams, later a star of *Roots*.

With a candelabrum on top of the piano, a toothy smile, and a head full of blond locks, Liberace was television's most appealing romantic figure—at least for the Geritol set—in the early 1950s.

Every misogynist's fantasy—that was *The Dean Martin Show*. Jerry Lewis's former partner *(right)* combined cigarettes, booze, and a group of women called "The Golddiggers." Martin made a virtue out of his lack of preparation and his casual approach to cues, jokes, and timing. In late 1966, Dean Martin gave a "hoe-down" *(above)* with an unusual guest list: (from left) Jane Powell, Liberace, Tennessee Ernie Ford, and Barbara McNair.

Singer Andy Williams *(left)* hosted a variety show in the tradition of Perry Como on NBC for several years in the 1960s and early 1970s. The Osmond Brothers *(above)* were regular performers on the show. The youngest one, Donny, on the far right, became cohost of *Donny & Marie* on ABC in 1976.

One of the first variety shows on television, starring one of the greats, Jimmy Durante, was *The All-Star Revue* on NBC. Durante's partner, Eddie Jackson ("Of Clayton, Jackson, and Du-rante!"), is seen here.

A variety show that begins at one o'clock in the morning? If it's rock 'n' roll music, appealing to partying youths, why not? Regular host Wolfman Jack *(left)* is shown here, along with the popular act Seals and Crofts *(below)*.

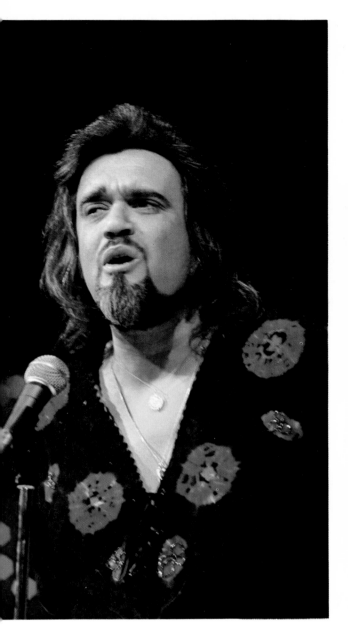

A direct descendant of *Major Bowes and His Original Amateur Hour*, *Ted Mack and the Original Amateur Hour* stayed on the air for twenty-two years, featuring tap dancers, accordion players, and other greats from America's heartland.

In June, 1953, the Ford Motor Company celebrated its fiftieth anniversary with a show telecast on both CBS and NBC. The lavish special was and is best remembered for the pairing of two of Broadway's biggest musical stars, Mary Martin and Ethel Merman. They demonstrated that none of the special visual effects of TV could match pure talent as a means of creating viewer excitement.

Two extraordinary singing talents join forces on a 1967 *Kraft Music Hall* presentation: Liza Minnelli and the late Bobby Darin.

Satire is what closes on Saturday night—so goes an old Broadway adage. An attempt to import a British satirical show, *That Was the Week That Was (opposite page, top, left),* failed in the mid-1960s. Later, public television brought over the madness of *Monty Python's Flying Circus (above)* to an enthusiastic audience. Here, playing the Dinsdale Brothers, are (from left) John Cleese, Michael Palin, Graham Chapman, Eric Idle, and Terry Jones. In 1975, NBC gave over the late-night Saturday slot to *Saturday Night,* an irreverent, frequently outrageous satirical show. Chevy Chase *(opposite page, top, right)*, here reading the improbable news of the week, gained fame as an impersonator of President Ford. The *Saturday Night* regulars *(right)* are (from left) Danny Aykroyd, Jane Curtin, Garrett Morris, Laraine Newman, Gilda Radner, Bill Murray, and John Belushi (who also appears below).

In addition to starring in a successful variety show, Carol Burnett teamed up with other performers to create memorable specials. Julie Andrews *(below)* and opera star Beverly Sills *(left)* were two of her favorite companions.

◄ His politics are strictly conservative Republican, and he turned his military tours into political statements, but Bob Hope was still a widely popular figure, in large measure due to his frequent tours of American military bases abroad. He's shown here in a 1967 Christmas visit to Vietnam.

This 1967 special, "Sinatra: A Man and His Music," shows what television can do when it stays away from cloying cuteness and lets two great performers perform. Just Sinatra, Ella Fitzgerald, and songs.

Fred Astaire and Barrie Chase *(left)* dance together on this 1968 NBC special. Dancers did not appear as regular television performers, but specials made room for them. Ann-Margret *(right)* displays a different dance style in this 1976 NBC show.

The Academy Awards, symbol of the movie industry which once regarded television with such fear, has become an annual production spectacular, and one of the most popular shows of the year. This dazzling production number *(left)* starring the late Rosalind Russell was in the 1973 awards ceremony. The Oscar set *(above)* appeared in 1975. For all the lavishly spent dollars, however, one of the charms of the Academy Awards is that it is live; there is always the possibility of the unexpected. In 1973, Sacheen Littlefeather *(right)* accepted Marlon Brando's Academy Award with a speech on Indian rights.

From instant to permanent fame: Phyllis George, crowned Miss America in 1971 by the immortal
Bert Parks, joined CBS to become the first successful female network sports announcer.

The more television broadcast parades, the more parades reshaped themselves to televisio
taste—with prerecorded production numbers and increasingly colorful and elaborate floats. T
New York Thanksgiving Day parade *(above)*, sponsored by Macy's, came to be primarily a
attraction. And the Rose Bowl parade *(below)*, narrated in 1976 by John Davidson and West Co
newscaster Kelly Lange, turned to elaborate scripts and "clever" patter to rouse New Year's revele

Composer-conductor Leonard Bernstein was a familiar sight on CBS on Sunday afternoons, explaining classical music to young viewers with a mixture of pedagogy and theatricality on *Young People's Concerts*.

The Bell Telephone Hour was a rare prime-time oasis of music, from popular to classical. Harry Belafonte *(left)* performed in this April, 1965, special, while Pablo Casals *(above)* played and conducted on another *Bell Telephone Hour,* in 1967.

The NBC Symphony Orchestra, an example of radio's partnership with serious music, was founded in 1937 under the baton of Arturo Toscanini. It survived into the television era, but after Toscanini's retirement in 1954 it was disbanded. And serious music all but disappeared from commercial television.

One of the traditions established by television was the musical version of *Peter Pan* with Mary Martin, presented by NBC in 1955, and shown for years after. The same network broadcast *Amahl and the Night Visitors (below)* in 1951, the first opera commissioned for television, written by Gian-Carlo Menotti. It was for fifteen years a traditional Christmastime presentation.

The longest-running musical in New York theater history, *The Fantasticks,* was presented on television by *The Hallmark Hall of Fame* in 1964. It featured Bert Lahr and Stanley Holloway as the perplexed fathers of the young lovers.

To present the Broadway play *High Button Shoes*, starring Phil Silvers, on television in 1948, cameras were simply placed in front of the stage.

Four long-distance runners: Bob Hope, Bing Crosby, John Wayne, and Frank Sinatra star in this 1975 comedy special.

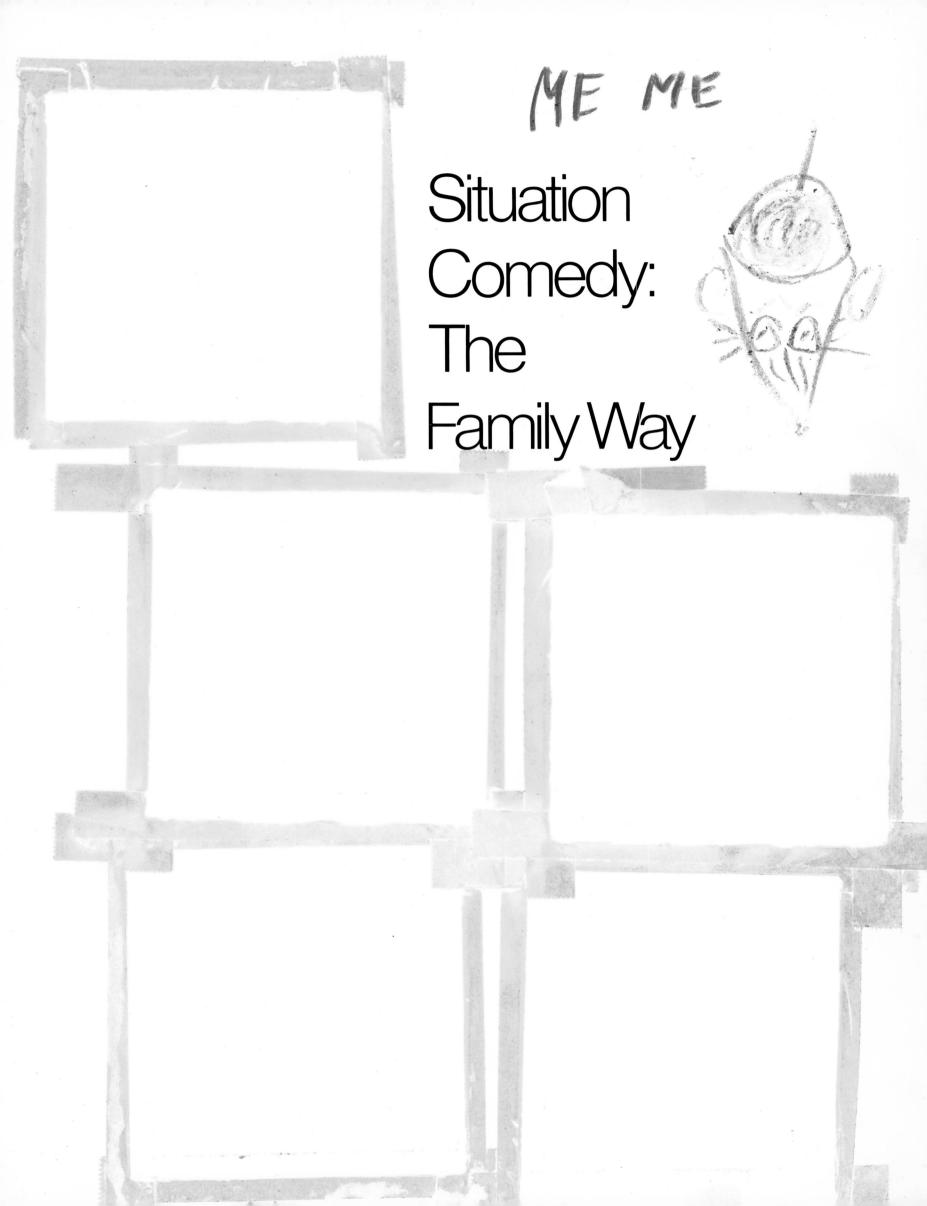

ME ME

Situation
Comedy:
The
Family Way

More than any other form, the situation comedy is the bedrock of regular American television. Variety shows have flourished and faded; dramatic shows have gone from live anthology presentations to filmed series, from cops to cowboys to doctors and back to cops; singers and bandleaders have long since been discarded by television programmers as prime-time stars. But the situation comedy has endured throughout television history—indeed, throughout broadcasting history— with the essential form all but untouched. The content has changed in the days from *I Love Lucy* to *The Mary Tyler Moore Show*, the subject matter has been broadened from *Fibber McGee and Molly* to *All in the Family* and *Maude,* but situation comedy has become the most predictable of prime-time offerings. And pre- dictability is precisely the reason for situation-comedy success. For these shows, virtually without exception, embody the central premise of American television programming: they give us characters whose habits, foibles, and responses to situations we know as we know those of our own friends and family. What's more, these characters—unlike real people—do not deviate from their habits. They provide a sense of family warmth without confusion, without ambiguity.

From the first days of network radio, situation comedy touched a nerve in the audience. In March of 1928, the National Broadcasting Company began broadcasting *Amos 'n' Andy*, a fifteen-minute show created and acted by Freeman Fisher Gosden and Charles J. Cor- rell. The show dealt with the comic adventures of a pair of South Side Chicago Negroes who ran the Fresh Air Taxi Cab Company of America, "Incorpulated," and whose social life revolved around the Mystic Knights of the Sea lodge, presided over by the Kingfish.

Most current observers who look back on *Amos 'n' Andy* see it as a mean-spirited exploitation of racial stereotypes. And, indeed, the mocking approach to black upward mobility, the mangling of the English lan- guage ("I'se re-*gusted*," "Splain dat to me"), and the fact that two white men played the Negro characters were all strong elements of racism. (The show was moved to television in 1951, with a black cast—Tim Moore as the Kingfish displayed a brilliant comedic

Two miscreants in search of adventure, wealth, or just some peace and quiet: it was the premise of the first broadcast situation comedy, *Amos 'n' Andy*, a huge radio success and long a hardy perennial. Freeman Gosden and Charles Correll, both white, played the two on radio.

Amos 'n' Andy's formula of pairing two trouble-prone males was often employed. Jackie Gleason and Art Carney in *The Honeymooners (right)* worked their mischief under the suspicious gaze of Audrey Meadows as Alice Kramden. Abbott and Costello *(far right)* were paired on NBC in the early days of television, and they are still seen in reruns. A more contemporary example *(farthest right)* is the television version of Neil Simon's hit play, *The Odd Couple*, with Tony Randall (right) and Jack Klugman. (Later the ladies got into the act, as in *Laverne & Shirley*.)

hand—but the growing anger over black stereotyping drove the show off the air and ultimately out of syndication by 1966.) More significant is the fact that this first broadcasting sit-com hit contained many of the ingredients that remain a part of the form almost fifty years later.

The characters are in a situation which is in essence unchanging. The taxicab company will *always* be a laughably small enterprise, with a tiny office and a single chair. The grand dreams of Amos will always be laughably impossible to realize. Kingfish will always be the operator, looking for the quick deal, and Andy will always be his victim. The supporting characters—the awesomely stupid Lightnin', the pompous Lawyer Calhoun—will be exactly the same, day in and day out. Even the vocabulary, the phrases used by the characters, will remain unvarying.

These elements remain intact no matter which situation comedy is examined. Many of them—*The Honeymooners*, with Jackie Gleason, Art Carney, and Audrey Meadows, to take a famous example—feature characters in economic straits who have dreams of success. A look at the apartment of Ralph and Alice Kramden reveals almost-desperate poverty: an ancient icebox, an old sink, a table with four chairs and always the same checked tablecloth, a bureau. Kramden is not content with his sorry lot: he is going to become a supervisor; he is going to get rich quick with a kitchen appliance; he is going to impress a wealthy acquaintance by socializing with him on the golf course.

The set-up—and the viewers' prior knowledge of the habits of these characters—establishes the humor. They know that Ed Norton will advise Kramden with a wild assortment of misinformation. They know that whenever Norton must write something, he will prepare for the task with an elaborate series of hand gestures, which will provoke Kramden to fury (*"Will you cut that out, Norton!?!"*). They know that Alice will be the voice of resigned reason, urging Ralph to reconsider his current scheme, and that they will clash ("One of these days . . . one of these days, Alice—*pow, right in the kisser!*"). They know that the plan will collapse as Kramden suffers the tortures of the damned (" . . . hamma, hamma, hamma . . ."), and that he will be consoled in the arms of his endlessly forgiving Alice ("Baby, you're the *greatest!*").

The utter predictability of what a character will do, given his habits, quirks, and foibles, far from boring the

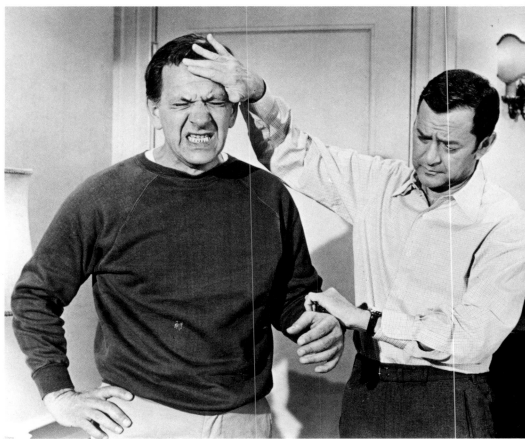

listening or viewing audience enriches the humor, because it brings to any one joke or dilemma a knowledge of that character's response. One of the funniest single moments in broadcasting, which took place on Jack Benny's radio show, provides a classic example of an audience completing the joke through its expectations. Benny, who had long established himself as one of the world's stingiest human beings, is on his way home late at night when he is accosted by a holdup man.

"Your money or your life!" the robber demands.

And then there is silence. Long, long moments of silence. Well before the irrelevant punchline ("I'm *thinking,* I'm *thinking!*"), the audience dissolved in laughter, fully grasping the predicament of the lovable tightwad. Similarly, in the long-running radio show *Fibber McGee and Molly*, Fibber's casual line about looking for a missing object in his closet triggered a wave of laughter. The audience knew that the famous, overcrowded closet would dislodge a mountain of junk on Fibber's head as soon as he opened the door. It did not need the inevitable payoff, the cascade of debris, to trigger the laugh. The joke arises from the situation itself, from a clearly defined character confronting a problem—as writer-producer Carl Reiner put it, "the interplay of situation and character." That is why, he said, "if someone asked me what was the best comedy line I have ever written, I would have to say it was probably a line like 'I see,' or 'Ah-hah!'"

The requirement of situation comedy, then, is a set of characters that the audience will laugh at—and with—and care about. It's the *character* that's the key. Some of the most famous and well-liked entertainment figures of their time have failed to make a success out of situation comedies, because the audience could not be persuaded to care about them in the show's frame of reference. Stars such as Ray Bolger, Jack Lemmon, Bing Crosby, Ed Wynn, Ronald Colman, Gertrude Berg (in *Mrs. G Goes to College*, not *The Goldbergs*), Mickey Rooney, Pat O'Brien, Ezio Pinza, James Stewart, and Doris Day have been unable to transfer their popularity to the characters they were portraying.

Conversely, Lucille Ball, television's first situation-comedy superstar, managed to convince her television audience that she was the scatterbrained, childlike, troublemaking wife of a Cuban bandleader in *I Love Lucy*. As a movie actress, Lucille Ball frequently played glamorous, sophisticated women. The television audience, however, accepted her as a broad comic figure.

The all-time comedy queen of television was Lucille Ball. Beginning in 1951, she was a weekly performer on CBS for twenty-three years. Older television viewers remember her best in *I Love Lucy*, with Desi Arnaz as bandleader Ricky Ricardo, and Vivian Vance and William Frawley as neighbors Fred and Ethel Mertz. The show relied on a heavy dose of slapstick, at which Lucille Ball proved herself without peer. Of course it was unbelievable—but it was very funny.

It accepted her so thoroughly that in 1977, twenty-six years after *I Love Lucy* began on CBS, films of the original shows with Ball, Desi Arnaz, and Vivian Vance and William Frawley as the neighborly Fred and Ethel Mertz, are still running on local stations all over America.

So the question is, how do successful situation comedies win over audiences? How do they make us not simply laugh at comic antics, but care about the principal characters? To a remarkably uniform extent, the key device is the creation of a *family*—either in a home situation, a work situation, or both—that bonds each character to the other, and, in turn, bonds the audience to the characters. The familial bond in situation comedy exists for the same reason that so many characters in dramatic series live alone. The goal in dramatic series is to forge a bond between audience and character that rises out of concern, fear, jeopardy. The viewers are his only companions in his battle against evil or disease or danger. In situation comedy, loneliness is anathema. Not only is there no one to "play off," no ready source of comic conflict, there is also no fundamental sense of security that underlies the dilemma in which a comic figure finds himself or herself. There must be someone—family or friends who act as family—to ease

the troubles of a comic figure with a comforting word or sense of concern.

The familial bond in situation comedy is all but total. Television comedy that has tried to make people laugh without the "safety net" of continuing, sympathetic characters has as a rule failed to attract a sufficient audience to enable it to survive, no matter how brilliant. Ernie Kovacs, the mad video genius of the 1950s and early 1960s who made the technology of television work as his humorous frame of reference, earned the distinction of having shows canceled by four television networks—CBS, ABC, NBC, and the now-defunct Du Mont television network. His inventiveness is legendary: musical pieces "played" by household appliances and foods; people vanishing in midair, or suddenly "shrunk" against giant pencils; tilted sets "straightened" by camerawork, so that olives rolled off "even" tables and milk poured crazily out of a thermos bottle. But the comedy of Kovacs could no more be contained in a series format than it could be explained by still photographs. It was comedy beyond the boundaries of a series, or even of a variety show with conventional skits. And it never found a mass audience.

More important, it is impossible to list a single situa-

No pretense of "reality" with vaudevillians George Burns and Gracie Allen in *The George Burns and Gracie Allen Show;* Burns would often interrupt the "plot" to make a few observations, punctuated by the ever-present cigar. Harry Von Zell, the show's announcer (left), was also the comic foil.

tion comedy where a single lead character confronted the world; it simply is not the way the genre works. The familial bond forms an unbroken chain from the earliest days of radio, through *Life of Riley* and *The Dick Van Dyke Show*, to the most "daring" comedies of Norman Lear. Whatever the controversial nature of the topics treated in contemporary comedies—abortion, impotence, menopause, homosexuality—no producer has as yet dared to break with the form of a close-knit, family-style relationship. At times, in fact, comedies make deliberate adjustments in order to create a closer relationship between characters.

In its first year and a half, for example, the ABC comedy *Happy Days* was a "marginal" show; its ratings, while adequate, did not insure its survival. The core of this recollection of teenage life in the 1950s was the Cunningham family, an agonizingly normal archeological dig: pudgy, hapless father; wise, everything-will-be-all-right mother; an overachieving Henry Aldrich of a teenage son; and a kid sister. The spice in the stew was

◄ Women in early television were locked into traditional roles, but they weren't always docile. Eve Arden, in *Our Miss Brooks (left)*, portrayed a sharp-tongued schoolteacher who drove the principal, played by Gale Gordon, to distraction. Ann Sothern *(below, left)* played Don Porter's acerbic *Private Secretary* (on the right is Joel Grey). By contrast, a modern situation-comedy woman, *Phyllis (bottom, left)*, played by Cloris Leachman (shown with guest star Robert Alda and regular Henry Jones), spent an uneasy two years searching for a job and a proper comic balance.

These are two different situation-comedy families. William Bendix, who inherited the title role from Jackie Gleason in *Life of Riley (top)*, was a paradigm dumb father, given to moaning "What a revoltin' development *this* is" at every crisis. His family included (from right) Marjorie Reynolds, Lugene Sanders, and Wesley Morgan. More than a decade later, *The Dick Van Dyke Show (above)* starred Van Dyke (far left) as a successful comedy writer, married to Mary Tyler Moore (far right). Morey Amsterdam and Rose Marie, his writer-colleagues and friends, provided the broader comic relief.

Two escapist views of youth: *Dobie Gillis (below)* was adapted from Max Shulman's stories of campus life in the late 1930s, updated to the late 1950s. Dwayne Hickman (second from left) played Dobie, with Bob Denver as his beatnik friend Maynard (far left), Sheila James as a girl nursing an unrequited love for Dobie, and Stephen Franken as rich snob Chatsworth Osborne, Jr. In 1975, ABC launched *Welcome Back, Kotter (right)*. Gabriel Kaplan plays the teacher who presides over the lovable antics of Barbarino (John Travolta), Washington (Lawrence Hilton-Jacobs), Epstein (Robert Hegyes), and Horshack (Ron Palillo). Marcia Strassman plays Kotter's wife, and John Sylvester White portrays Mr. Woodman.

the motorcycle-driving Arthur Fonzarelli, a super-cool defanged Wild One who knew the deepest mysteries of women and the art of being Cool. The problem was that Fonzarelli—"The Fonz"—was an outsider with no family bond and no ties to anyone else in the show except when he assumed the role of teacher to the unsophisticated teenagers.

So, in the fall of 1975, *Happy Days* creator Garry Marshall changed the show by having The Fonz rent out the attic apartment above the Cunninghams' garage, thus making him a surrogate member of the family.

"I knew," Marshall recalled after the show had become the number-one regular series in the ratings, "that if I got him over the garage, I could get him into the kitchen; he could 'become' a member of the family."

The first show of that season featured The Fonz losing his cool and approaching tears as he explained to the Cunninghams that he'd never known a real family before. That confession convinced the reluctant father to rent Fonzie the room, and helped to humanize the character, tempering his "cool" with vulnerability. It was also the beginning of the shift of Henry Winkler's "Fonzie" from a fairly popular supporting character in a

marginal television show to a national folk hero in the most popular show in America.

If there is one consistently dishonest element in every situation comedy, no matter how realistic, how bold, how relevant or controversial it may be, it is that no one in a situation comedy is isolated, alone, atomized. In a country where family bonds are dissolving, where broken marriages are increasing almost geometrically, and where the trend of living alone is becoming an important national fact of life, the world of the situation comedy depicts strong bonds between friends, coworkers, and family. No one sits home at night watching television; the most pervasive habit in American life today usually goes unrecorded in even the most "realistic" comedies because it is not funny. Instead, the sturdiest barriers of isolation vanish under the power of the family bond. The students of Gabe Kotter in *Welcome Back, Kotter* pal around together—an Italian, a black, a Puerto Rican Jew, a white eastern European ethnic—in a poverty-stricken neighborhood in Brooklyn where, in reality, racial polarization has been at a flash point for a decade or more. And they frequently arrive, alone or together, at the apartment of their teacher, an event which, for

A television wedding is a sure tonic for the ratings. In one of the gentlest of early situation comedies *(below)*, Wally Cox as *Mr. Peepers* weds Patricia Benoit in 1954. Far left is Marion Lorne, a key supporting character. Not pictured is Tony Randall. In 1975, *Rhoda* (Valerie Harper) married Joe Gerard (David Groh) in a one-hour special *(left)* that won big ratings for CBS but sent the show off the tracks. A year later, Joe and Rhoda separated, and in the fall of 1977, they became divorced.

many New York teachers in such a neighborhood, would trigger an emergency call to the police. When *Rhoda* premiered on CBS in the fall of 1974, she was supposed to be a modern woman living alone; yet she moved into her sister's apartment. And when she was married off (under the push of then-CBS programming chief Fred Silverman, who wanted a ratings blockbuster), she managed to find an apartment in the same building as her sister. Even after its hit debut, *Laverne & Shirley* was changed to include the character of Laverne's father; a harassed, confused, but lovable pizza-parlor owner, he was an adult presence missing in the first season of the show.

So prevalent is the family in situation comedy that a stock opening line has become an industry joke as the symbol of the worn-out sit-com ("Hi, honey, I'm home!"). So concerned are producers and network programmers about preserving a family sensibility in the show that when sit-coms began to present one-parent families, the only safe explanation for the missing partner was death; divorce was considered unsettling. As late as 1975, NBC failed with *Fay,* a show about a vibrant woman in her forties who is in the process of discarding her husband and rediscovering her

Penny Marshall (left) as Laverne and Cindy Williams as Shirley are off on a frolic—disguised as men to erase their phone number scrawled on a men's room wall. Shortly after the hit series began in early 1976, Phil Foster arrived as Laverne's father to increase the show's "familial" quality.

111

Beneath the yelling, the screaming, the insults, and the imprecations are warm family ties. *All in the Family (left)*, the 1971 Norman Lear show that began the trend toward "realism" in sit-coms, binds (from left) Jean Stapleton (Edith Bunker), Sally Struthers (Gloria Stivic), Rob Reiner (Mike Stivic), and Carroll O'Connor (Archie Bunker), into a close family unit. If the kids hate the grownups, why are they living next door? Similarly *(below, left)*, however much Fred Sanford (Redd Foxx) dissembles to his son (Demond Wilson), they stand together to preserve their junkyard and their independence. A James Komack reworking of the *Sanford and Son* format, *Chico and the Man (below, right)*, tied Jack Albertson and Freddie Prinze into a similar bond, despite Albertson's racial assaults. Real life is not so kind: Freddie Prinze committed suicide in 1977. Foxx broke up his "family" by moving to ABC.

own life and lusts. After two network airings, the show was canceled—in part because the network's research found audiences uncomfortable with the situation. Fay's estranged husband would often be a part of the setting, asking her to try again. As a comic device, the relationship between Lee Grant and Joe Silver often worked well; as a warm-hearted family arrangement, it was confusing, ambiguous. It did not work. (*One Day At a Time,* with a divorcee as the main character, has won good ratings, but here the woman lives with two teenage daughters.)

In contrast, consider the comedies of Norman Lear. Beginning with *All in the Family* and continuing through *Maude* and *Good Times,* Lear's comedies have often been called breakthroughs, and they have often used words and topics long considered taboo. Archie Bunker, the lead in Lear's first success, *All in the Family,* is a bigot who employs terms such as "black beauties" to describe blacks, "dagoes" for Italians, and similar expressions of nonendearment. From its debut, the show used the sexual appetite of the Bunkers' daughter and son-in-law for comic effect, and also devoted a show to the temporary impotence of the son-in-law. Edith Bunker went through menopause; a hero-athlete Archie knew turned out to be gay; a woman he encountered was really a transvestite male. Maude got pregnant and had an abortion; she and her husband went through a lengthy separation. The Evans family in *Good Times* lives in a Chicago housing project in the ghetto, and shows have touched on teenage alcoholism and the desperate efforts of the family to escape ceaseless poverty.

But the family ties in Norman Lear's comedies are thoroughly conventional, thoroughly middle American; they represent not a departure from the situation comedies of the past but an affirmation of the form. Archie Bunker is, in his own way, devoted to his wife and daughter and susceptible of emotional vulnerability (he is a far cry from his British inspiration, Alf Garnett of *Till Death Do Us Part,* whose bigotry, misogyny, and general meanness of spirit is mercilessly consistent). For all his fulminations against his "meathead" son-in-law, Mike and Gloria lived for years under the same roof as the Bunkers, and when they became parents of Archie's grandchild, they moved next door: not precisely the goal of a contemporary young couple of liberal political and sexual persuasion.

In *Good Times* and *The Jeffersons,* the fact that the principal characters are black is interesting, but not nearly as important as their embodiment of traditional values and their strong sense of family. Until the father

Beatrice Arthur and Bill Macy portray a modern, compulsively neurotic couple in *Maude;* he drinks, she screams, they fight, they even separate. But the family unit remains.

figure in *Good Times,* played by John Amos, was killed off at the start of the 1976 season because of Amos's contractual dispute with Lear, the father was a powerful center of the family, with middle-class aspirations. He was a strong parental presence, a dispenser of strict, corporal discipline; he insisted that his children stay in school, that they abide by the law. George Jefferson is the man who made it: an affluent man who dresses like a yacht club executive in his off-hours, he aspires to join the social elite, while his exasperated but loving wife reminds him of his ghetto origins. Both of these shows—in fact, all of Lear's network offerings—insist on the family as the source of strength and ethical values (*Mary Hartman, Mary Hartman* takes a more jaded view of home and hearth, which may be one reason why all three networks rejected it). And all of these shows, however precedent-shattering they are in confronting *issues,* resolve them with a return inward to the family. *Good Times* may be an ironic title given the characters' lifestyle of poverty, but the family is a center of warmth, love, and humor. As ABC's research vice-president, Marvin Mord, once observed, "the people in that show are *very happy* people."

Even in shows where the "family" is absent, the bond is very strong. *The Mary Tyler Moore Show* broke a lot of rules by presenting a young woman who lived alone, who was unmarried, and whose dates did not stop at the apartment door. Her parents were far away; there was no happy brood with whom she boarded. This show, however, provided a familial bond through the workplace. Lou Grant, Murray Slaughter, even the laughable Ted Baxter were frequent visitors in each other's homes, and provided each other a shoulder to cry on, a hearing for grievances and pains. At home, there was Rhoda Morgenstern for sympathy and a dash of spice to counter Mary's originally sugary soul, and Phyllis Lindstrom for the vinegar (when Phyllis was spun off in her cwn show, Sue Ann Nivens, the "Happy Homemaker," was built up to provide the antidote of bitchiness to Mary's personality).

Sometimes the work family can erase the need for a more conventional family bond. In *Barney Miller*, the men (and token women) of the precinct house provide the tie; Barney Miller's wife became so irrelevant that she was written out of the show. And the ravages of war make a real family impossible on *M*A*S*H*; instead, the company works as a family, from the fatherly colonel to the kid brother (Radar). No matter what the situation, no matter how independent they may seem, the show follows the unbreakable sit-com rule: do not leave these characters to face the world alone.

Aside from the standard requirement of a strong family composed of characters who will elicit audience involvement, situation comedy reflects another consistent pattern. What emerges is a kind of delayed-reaction portrayal of these familial bonds. Television life in situation comedy—not always, but often—reflects not "the way we live now," but the way we lived a few years ago. It's almost as if television in situation comedy is trying to put back into the American home those qualities that are no longer there; this is also true

In *The Mary Tyler Moore Show*, Mary's status as a single woman is balanced by the strong, familial ties at the office. She's shown *(left)* during a temporary spat with newswriter Murray Slaughter, played by Gavin MacLeod, with Ted Baxter (Ted Knight) in the middle. Bob Newhart, playing a psychologist married to Suzanne Pleshette in *The Bob Newhart Show (right)*, cares for two "families"—the office crowd, and the childlike neighbor Howard (played by Bill Daily). ABC's *Barney Miller (below)* offers a close-knit unit of police detectives nicely spiced for ethnic diversity: "Wojo" (Maxwell Gail), Miller (Hal Linden), Harris (Ron Glass), Fish (Abe Vigoda), and Yemana (Jack Soo). Barbara Barrie, who played Miller's wife, was retired from the series, since she never really fit into the police "family."

A strong dose of ethnic characterizations found its way into early television shows via radio sit-coms, even as ethnic America was dispersing. Gertrude Berg's *The Goldbergs (top)* portrayed life in a loving Jewish home. Here, guest star Arthur Godfrey, center, surrounded by (from left) Eli Mintz, Arlene ("Fuzzy") McQuade, Larry Robinson, Gertrude Berg, and Philip Loeb, looks somewhat apprehensive as Molly Goldberg fills his plate. *I Remember Mama (center)*, starring Peggy Wood (far right), portrayed life in a loving Norwegian home. She shares a laugh here with the rest of the Hansen family—from left, Dick Van Patten, Judson Laire (as "Papa"), Robin Morgan, and Rosemary Rice. *Life with Father (bottom)*, adapted from the long-running Broadway show by Lindsay and Crouse, portrayed life in a loving WASP home. Leon Ames was Father (far left), and the family was played by (from left) Harvey Grant, Ralph Reed, Freddie Leiston, Ronald Keith, and Lurene Tuttle.

of dramatic series, in a different context, and especially true of television advertising.

Television's early days, for example, brought to the screen a number of video versions of radio comedies dealing with the adventures of big-city ethnic families, with strong ties to Old World customs and values; the clash of values between the parents and the more sophisticated, more "Americanized" daughters and sons was a basic comedic theme of these shows. They were Italian *(Life With Luigi)*, Scandinavian *(I Remember Mama)*, Jewish *(The Goldbergs)*—and they were on television at the very time when, at the end of World War II, the rush to the suburbs was unraveling these kinds of families, beginning to drain the life and vitality from "the old neighborhoods."

The 1950s was a time when the "disappearing father" was a growing reality. In part because of the commuting distances between city and suburb, in part because of the movement into the white-collar class and the longer working hours that move required, in part because the small, family-owned and -operated shops were disappearing, the father figure was not home as often. And in the fifties there appeared—in contrast to popular nostalgic memory—not only the bumbling, ludicrous father image of Chester A. Riley (as played first by Jackie Gleason and then by William Bendix) or the amnesiac Stu Erwin in *Trouble with Father*, but a kind, concerned, and *ever-present* father. The laughs might be broad, as in Danny Thomas's *Make Room for Daddy* (later *The Danny Thomas Show*); they might be quiet, as in *Father Knows Best*; or they might be supplied wholly by a mechanical laugh track, as in *The Adventures of Ozzie and Harriet* (ABC's first successful situation comedy—and its only one for

Although fathers were spending less time at home in the late fifties, you'd never know it from these sit-coms. Danny Thomas, in *Make Room for Daddy*, later *The Danny Thomas Show (above)*, was frequently exasperated by his family, but he was always there to remind them of the proper moral principles, usually offered with the subtlety of a twenty-pound sledgehammer. Thomas is shown here with Angela Cartwright as his daughter, Marjorie Lord as his wife, Rusty Hamer as his son, and series regulars Pat Carroll and Sid Melton. Robert Young was the ever-calm father of *Father Knows Best (above, right)*, shepherding (on stairs, from left) Elinor Donahue, Billy Gray, and Lauren Chapin through life. Jane Wyatt played his wife. Raised voices? Violent family quarrels? No chance. Ozzie, Harriet *(right)*, Rick *(below)*, and Dave Nelson played—Ozzie, Harriet, Rick, and Dave, moving through life with the turbulence of a boat on a molasses-filled lake. What Ozzie did for a living was never divulged, but, based on his presence at home, the hours were right.

In these three examples of family comedy, the comedy was often all but invisible. In *My Three Sons (above, right)*, Fred MacMurray played Steve Douglas, at first a widower, assisted by Uncle Charlie (William Demarest) in rearing his three sons, only one of whom, Chip (Barry Livingston), is pictured here, along with the second wife (Beverly Garland), Dodie (Dawn Lyn), and Tramp. "I'm worried about the Beaver, Ward," Barbara Billingsley said to Hugh Beaumont *(above, left)* in *Leave It to Beaver*. Why? Big brother Wally (Tony Dow) didn't even wear sideburns. If one "father" (Brian Keith) isn't enough, how about two? Sebastian Cabot played the ever-present Giles French in *A Family Affair (below)*, a long-running CBS comedy. Johnny Whitaker, Anissa Jones, and Kathy Garver were their wards.

many years). But whatever the quality of the humor, these fathers were always there to listen to the problems of their children, to offer advice, to express concern ("I'm worried about the Beaver, Ward." "Mmmmm. Why?"). These men never seemed to be out of town or distracted by work pressures. In fact, it was impossible to figure out what Ozzie Nelson did at all besides sit in the living room waiting for Rick or David to come in with a domestic dilemma.

In the early 1960s, the American political tensions began to increase. The civil-rights movement began hitting the headlines; there were riots in New York City in 1964, fire hoses and police dogs in Birmingham, Alabama, in 1963 and in Selma, Alabama, in 1965. At first peacefully with sit-ins in 1961, then more divisively with Berkeley in 1964, signs that the younger generation was stirring appeared. During this time and throughout the later 1960s, the most successful string of situation comedies were CBS's rural, "hick" comedies, celebrating the values of small-town life. ABC actually began the form with *The Real McCoys* in 1957, starring Walter Brennan, Richard Crenna, and Kathleen Nolan as a family of self-reliant hillbillies. But it was *The Beverly Hillbillies*, featuring a family of mountain folk that struck it rich, moved to Beverly Hills, but kept its customs and values intact, that signaled the trend when it began on CBS in 1962. It is true, as David Boroff has written, that the show "offers the standard myths of populist reassurance: the superior wisdom of the unlettered; the fecklessness of the upper class, the gaiety of the ignorant, the pompous solemnity of the rich." It was in fact the city-slicker-bested-by-the-country-bumpkin routine.

But it was also an escape route out of the increasing-

Walter Brennan as grandpappy Amos and Richard Crenna as Luke *(above)* starred in the 1957 rural-comedy forerunner, *The Real McCoys*. The brood was big, fun-loving, and closely knit. Now take such a family, move them to corrupt, sophisticated Beverly Hills, preserve their traditions and simplicity, and what do you have? You have *The Beverly Hillbillies*, from 1962 to 1972 one of the most popular rural comedies *(top)*. Irene Ryan and Buddy Ebsen kept the younger members of the clan, Donna Douglas and Max Baer, in line.

The Andy Griffith Show, starring Griffith, Don Knotts, Ron Howard (later of *Happy Days*), and Frances Bavier, was another popular rural comedy, which spun off *Gomer Pyle—USMC* and *Mayberry R.F.D.*, perfect antidotes to the clamorous 1960s.

ly difficult problems of discordant urban America. Along with its progeny—*Green Acres, The Andy Griffith Show, Petticoat Junction, Mayberry R.F.D.*—the show conjured up a way of life that did not require tranquilizers, that no urbanized black or civil-rights agitator could penetrate.

And during this same period in which America was growing quarrelsome with itself appeared another sitcom trend: the fantasy escape. *Bewitched, I Dream of Jeannie, My Favorite Martian, The Munsters, The Addams Family, My Mother the Car, My Living Doll, Mister Ed, Gilligan's Island* all began in the first half of the 1960s. All of them featured—through friendly ghouls, enchanted spells, or a fortuitous shipwreck—complete escape from the realities of American life.

The comedy that "broke the rules" of noncontroversial situation comedies, showing clashes between older and younger generations, between black and white, and between ethnic and WASP, did not air on CBS in the last half of the 1960s, when campuses and cities were in flames, when the war in Vietnam—and controversy over its handling—was at its peak. *All in the Family* had its premiere in January, 1971—when the passions were cooling down. Sometime between the Democratic National Convention of 1968 and the shootings at Kent State and Jackson State colleges in 1970, the tensions had erupted, then subsided. Only then—not when the divisiveness was strongest—could a comic treatment of still-existing serious divisions win mass audience acceptance.

Perhaps it takes time for writers, producers, and networks to absorb the currents in American life; perhaps they know, by instinct or by research, that it's important to let the currents ebb before presenting them in a comic frame of reference. Or perhaps ABC vice-president Bob Shanks, in his book *The Cool Fire*, explains why even out-of-phase reality works in comic, but not dramatic situations:

We have been through the bruising sixties, when every issue was dragged kicking and screaming into the light, when every value, supposedly fixed in granite, was challenged and frequently seen to be made of chalk. . . . In the numbing and more resigned seventies, audiences know, and know that everybody else knows, what all the difficult, even insoluble problems are. What does one do in such cases? Laugh.

What to make of all of this? If you are devising a drama, make it escapist; if you are creating a comedy, make it real . . . cartoon real.

One of the earliest—and best—fantasy sit-coms was *Topper (above)*, starring Leo G. Carroll as the stuffy Cosmo Topper, haunted by fun-loving ghosts Anne Jeffreys and Robert Sterling. *I Dream of Jeannie (below)* starred Barbara Eden as a sex object, and Larry Hagman *(left)* as her befuddled "master," shown here with Sammy Davis, Jr. *The Munsters (top, right)*, a misunderstood family of ghouls, starred Yvonne De Carlo and Fred Gwynne. *My Mother the Car (bottom)* starred Jerry Van Dyke *(right)*, here pictured with Avery Schreiber. Ann Sothern was the voice of Jerry's mother, reincarnated as an automobile. Alan Young *(bottom, right)* was the human friend of a talking horse in *Mister Ed*. The animal in *Bewitched (right, center)* is only visiting; Elizabeth Montgomery, the star, is shown with Maurice Evans.

Another handy route to escape is to maroon your characters on a desert island. Bob Denver (front, wearing a sailor cap) was Gilligan, supported by (from left) Russell Johnson, Alan Hale, Dawn Wells, Tina Louise, Jim Backus, and Natalie Schafer. *Gilligan's Island* is often ranked with *My Mother the Car* in the annals of absurd situation comedies.

Don Adams (right) as Maxwell Smart, Agent 86, and Barbara Feldon as Agent 99 confront "The Chief," played by Edward C. Platt, in *Get Smart!*, a parody of the James Bond genre that surfaced in dramatic television shows of the 1960s. This show, created by Buck Henry and Mel Brooks, sent several catchphrases into the culture: "Sorry about that" and "Would you believe . . . ?" among them.

One of the few attempts to speak to the growing rock culture of the sixties was *The Monkees*, modeled after the music and film style of the Beatles (from left, Peter Tork, David Jones, and Mike Nesmith are shown; Micky Dolenz is in the bushes). The music was created in the studio.

Besides the obvious use of the familial ties such a life enforces, how is the military treated in situation comedy? In *You'll Never Get Rich (bottom)*, a brilliant writing team headed by the late Nat Hiken and a brilliant cast headed by Phil Silvers (shown here along with Harvey Lembeck, second from left, Maurice Gosfield, far right, and other members of Company B) created some of the finest sit-com moments. In *Hogan's Heroes (below)*, Allied prisoners of war in World War II, led by Bob Crane, foreground, played Dead End Kids to laughable Nazis (Werner Klemperer, left, Cynthia Lyn, and John Banner); the premise unsettled many. *Gomer Pyle—USMC (right)* starred Jim Nabors and Frank Sutton in a show that, in its attempt to avoid any social comment, succeeded admirably.

(Shanks also predicted that silliness would soon be coming back; in the light of *Laverne & Shirley, Welcome Back, Kotter*, and other ABC comic offerings, this prediction makes him a prophet with honor at his own network.)

None of these points is to deny the skills that can make a television comedy as funny as a good Broadway show. The old Phil Silvers show, *You'll Never Get Rich*, featuring Sgt. Bilko's platoon pitted against the bureaucratic Colonel Hall, produced several comic gems. One of them, "The Court Martial," about a chimpanzee mistakenly inducted into the army during a manic attempt at efficiency, is a classic satire on bureaucracy. The first *Dick Van Dyke Show*, created by Carl Reiner and featuring the first-rate comic cast of Van Dyke, Mary Tyler Moore, Morey Amsterdam, and Rose Marie, was a flawlessly played light comedy. Many of Lear's shows, and those of MTM Productions, work as entertainment and as often touching character sketches. In particular, *The Mary Tyler Moore Show* bent the immobile character forms: Lou Grant, the newsroom boss, lost his wife to divorce and remarriage; he became, in the words of one of the show's creators, "a casualty of the feminist revolution." Mary became more assertive, less the country girl lost in the big city. *M*A*S*H*, the bittersweet comedy set in the Korean War, has proved that the sit-com form can not only be bent, but also broken, provided the audience knows what the situation is (men and women under siege), and who the characters are. The show has often dropped the element of "comedy" completely, dealing instead with the horror of young men dying in combat.

M*A*S*H*, which began in 1972, broke many of the rules of situation comedies. By maintaining a high level of writing and acting, and by having the good sense to link a brilliant actor (Alan Alda as Hawkeye) with a brilliant executive producer-director (Larry Gelbart), *M*A*S*H** became the most honest and outspoken of all situation comedies. It survived frequent changes in time periods and cast members. The original cast *(left)* featured (front row, from left) Wayne Rogers as Trapper, Alan Alda as Hawkeye, McLean Stevenson as Colonel Henry Blake, and Gary Burghoff as Radar. In rear are "Hot Lips" Houlihan (Loretta Swit) and Major Frank Burns (Larry Linville). Colonel Potter (Harry Morgan, seated at desk) took command *(below)* from Henry, and Captain B. J. Hunnicutt (Mike Farrell, third from right) replaced Trapper. Also shown is Father Mulcahy (William Christopher).

Two examples of early sit-com stereotyping are shown here. In *My Little Margie (left)*, Gale Storm played a scatterbrained adult woman who bedeviled her father (Charles Farrell, left); her brains were matched by those of her boyfriend Freddie (Don Hayden). In *Beulah (right)*, a succession of black actresses—this one is Louise Beavers (left), pictured with Ruby Dandridge—showed how happy life as a domestic could be.

Sometimes there is no "situation," only a series of vignettes as recounted by Hawkeye in his letters home. In one episode, built around the premise of an American television reporter interviewing the people of the MASH unit, the entire show was shot in black-and-white—as it would have appeared on television in the early 1950s—and the actors improvised their responses to the questions, talking about fear and anger and horror under the conditions of war.

It is also clearly true that situation comedy today is not simply more realistic about topics, but also about people. The comedies of the first twenty years of commercial television—almost without exception—were monolithic in their representation of prevailing cultural values. Women stayed at home or worked in role-defined jobs such as secretary, teacher, and model; and while millions of women were entering the work force in the 1950s and 1960s, television treated the idea that a woman might go to work while a man stayed home and cared for the children as a comic device. People, particularly the women of such shows as *I Love Lucy* and *My Little Margie*, were children—manipulative, lying, deceptive, constitutionally unable to say to husband or father, "I know you're bringing the boss home for dinner, but I burned the roast, so let's go out

to eat." Instead, twenty-one minutes of deception was required. Blacks in those television shows were either invisible or played as complete stereotypes: Willie Best portrayed the bug-eyed elevator operator on *My Little Margie*, Ethel Waters (and Hattie McDaniel and Louise Beavers) played the happy-go-lucky domestic on *Beulah*, and not until the 1968 airing of *Julia* on NBC did a network cast a black as a leading figure (though how the character, ostensibly a nurse, could afford an apartment and wardrobe more suitable to a corporate vice-president was never explained).

Situation comedy today is in *its* "golden age." It is more honest and funnier than it has ever been, and gives a more accurate portrayal of American life than do most serious shows. What this suggests is that the viewing audience is prepared to accept some unpleasant or divisive topics—provided the context itself is comfortable and relatively reassuring. Once we know that these characters are endearing (despite their prejudices or shortcomings), once we know that they are safe from the ravages of loneliness and abandonment, once we know that they are protected by the kinds of roots most Americans seem to be longing for, we can laugh with them and cry with them, secure in their own warm, protective familial bond.

Drama and Adventure: What Happened to the "Golden Age"?

Margaret Sullavan starred in *The Storm* in 1948, the first production of *Studio One*, a CBS weekly anthology drama. *The Last Cruise*, a 1950 *Studio One* production, ventured to create visual excitement within the cramped limits of the studio.

Despite the enormous strides in technology which have considerably enlarged television's capabilities, many of the program forms of television have remained remarkably constant over the last thirty years. The early morning news shows, the late-night and midday talk shows, the network news, game shows, soap operas, and situation comedies—all have retained their essential shapes. The one television form that has changed almost completely from television's early days is the dramatic form.

It has changed production location: from New York to Los Angeles. It has changed texture: from live television to film. It has changed format: from the "anthology" series, presenting original works and dramatic adaptations covering a wide range of topics, to the continuing series, featuring characters whose vocations, surroundings, companions, and emotional responses are rigidly defined. (While these series have been supplemented over the last decade with the made-for-TV movie and the more recent concept of the "mini-series," continuing series are still the bedrock offerings of network television in the dramatic range.) It has changed content: from closeup emotional conflict emphasizing character, best suited to live, studio-originated shows, to physical conflict emphasizing action—fists, guns, cars, and explosives—best suited to film.

The reasons for these changes—a mix of economics, network competitiveness, advertising pressure, popular taste, and corporate timidity—tell much about the way the shape of television itself has changed since its introduction into American life almost thirty years ago. They also point to a structural conflict that is rooted in the very existence of a commercial broadcasting system: it is licensed by the government to serve the public interest, but operated by a cluster of private interests working to earn the biggest possible profit from a medium that cannot be expanded beyond the absolute limits of time.

The early days of television were characterized by conditions that helped to create the climate for a wide variety of relatively freewheeling television drama. First, all production originated in New York City, because that is where the headquarters of radio broadcasting were located, and that is where the networks established their experimental television studios: CBS in a Grand Central Station studio, NBC on the third floor of 30 Rockefeller Plaza. This meant that, by geographic proximity alone, the influence on television drama in the early days came from Broadway rather than Hollywood. The movie studios, in fact, regarded television as a mortal enemy, and refused to have anything to do with it during its first few years.

Second, in the late 1940s television was not truly a "mass medium." Even as late as 1950, only 4.4 million television sets had been purchased in America; the coaxial cable, permitting live television transmission across great distances, did not reach Chicago until 1949, and Los Angeles until 1951; many communities, especially in the mountain and western states, did not have access to television; and the initial high price of receivers made it at first a plaything of the relatively affluent. Nor were those first few years a source of great profit: through 1948, NBC was losing $13,000 a day on television. On the other hand, advertising rates were low: the same hour of studio time that cost $27,215 on network radio cost $1,510 on television. There was thus not much to lose in producing offbeat drama, either in terms of offending great masses or in risking huge amounts of money. And the very lack of alternatives, the dependence on live, studio production, made the dramatic play the most feasible form to present on television.

However much contemporary network programmers like to disparage "the Golden Age of television drama," however true it is that many of these early offerings were amateurishly written, directed, and acted, the fact is that television drama through the first decade of its existence was, by present standards, astonishingly di-

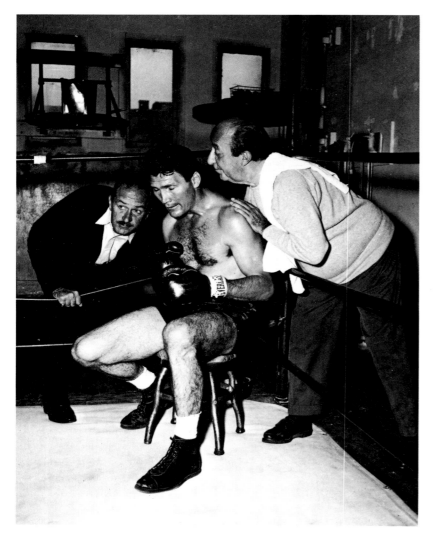

Du Pont Show of the Month provided outstanding dramas in the late 1950s. This production of *Wuthering Heights* in 1958 starred Richard Burton, Denholm Elliott (rear), and Yvonne Furneaux (shortly before the live airing of the show, she was replaced by Rosemary Harris).

verse. It began in May of 1947, with the premiere of *The Kraft Television Theatre* on NBC. It flourished with no less than eleven network anthology shows every week in the early 1950s, including *Studio One, The Philco-Goodyear Playhouse, The United States Steel Hour, Robert Montgomery Presents, Playhouse 90* (the only weekly entry to originate from California). It was buttressed by a series of less frequent dramatic shows: *Du Pont Show of the Month, The Hallmark Hall of Fame,* the frequent dramatic presentations on *Omnibus*. Its essential content, as one student of television, William Bluem, put it, "was anthology drama—stories of human conflict and confrontation, played with honesty and authority in living sight, sound, and motion before audiences the size of which no actor, writer, or director in all theatrical history would have dared to dream." There were, to be sure, times when the producers and directors of these early series sought to experiment with the limits of studio television. In 1956, *The Kraft Television Theatre* staged *A Night to Remember*, about the sinking of the *Titanic*, which required 107 actors, 31 sets, and 7 cameras. In 1959, when anthology drama was beginning to decline, *Playhouse 90* spent the then incredible

The Hollywood-based *Playhouse 90* attempted to preserve the New York tradition of live, original dramas. Its second show, Rod Serling's *Requiem for a Heavyweight (extreme left)*, was an outstanding production, starring Jack Palance, Keenan Wynn, and his father Ed Wynn. *Days of Wine and Roses (far left)*, a *Playhouse 90* original production written by J. P. Miller, starred Cliff Robertson, Piper Laurie, and Charles Bickford (not shown). In 1958, the show adapted Irwin Shaw's *Eighty-Yard Run (left)* into a drama starring Paul Newman (right) and Joanne Woodward, shown here with Richard Anderson.

One of the most ambitious efforts to program for a frankly "elitist" audience resulted in *Omnibus*, hosted by Alistair Cooke. The show appeared on each of the three commercial networks successively from 1952 to 1959. Here Cooke introduces the Broadway cast of *Oklahoma!*

In 1959, *Playhouse 90* mounted an expensive ($300,000) two-part taped production of Hemingway's *For Whom the Bell Tolls*, starring Jason Robards, Jr., and Maria Schell. It was a brave but futile attempt to preserve anthology drama as a regular feature of commercial television.

sum of $300,000 for a taped, two-part version of *For Whom the Bell Tolls*. Essentially, however, television drama was small-scale, tightly contained in space and scope, technically incapable of incorporating, for example, car chases, exploding warehouses, and chases down city streets. The focus had to be on people: what they said, what they thought, what they feared. And because television combined the closeup possibilities of film with the intangible magic of a live, this-is-it performance, television drama was able, as *Hallmark Hall of Fame* producer George Schaefer put it, "to catch the glowing, growing kind of performance you might see on the stage if you were a bumblebee buzzing around everywhere you wanted to be. This is a distinct contribution of television. In this unique way, the medium does something beyond the living stage, and something film can't do at all."

In sheer quantity, the live dramatic output of television was staggering. One study estimated that between 1950 and 1955, for just *three* weekly series, more than three hundred original hour-long plays were written and produced. These were not scripts written to order, based on preexisting characters, conflicts, or problems; they were plays written because the writer had something to say, and had an outlet where he was permitted to say it. As to quality, TV historians Arthur Shulman and Roger Youman, in their book *How Sweet It Was*, found that for one week in the fall of 1954 "one could see: 'Middle of the Night,' with E. G. Marshall and Eva Marie Saint; 'Twelve Angry Men,' with Franchot Tone; an adaptation of 'Lady in the Dark,' starring Ann Sothern; a play by Robert E. Sherwood . . . and a half-dozen others—all live, of course . . ." They found much the same pattern in 1955. And the measure of achievement is to be found less in the occasional spectacular triumph—Paddy Chayefsky's *Marty* with Rod Steiger and Nancy Marchand, Reginald Rose's *Twelve Angry Men*, Rod Serling's *Patterns*—than in the fact that every week there was room for the likes of Chayefsky, Rose, Serling, Tad Mosel, Robert Alan Aurthur, Gore Vidal, Calder Willingham, and other young, unknown writers. The anthologies also employed such directors as John Frankenheimer, Sidney Lumet, and George Roy Hill. Nor were these shows confined to an Eastern intellectual ghetto; as late as December, 1954, four of the ten top-rated shows were weekly anthology dramas.

What happened to the age of live, character-based, small-scale anthology drama? Television began to change as the medium began to grow and absorb everything in its path—especially its onetime rivals, the movie studios. Technology, economics, and simple fear combined to all but obliterate a once crucial element of commercial television.

First, look at some of the disadvantages of live television in the early days. The most obvious disadvantage was that it was a one-time-only proposition. For each week new sets, new costumes, new props were required. And as television costs grew, those expenses grew more burdensome. And since the technology of videotape recording was not perfected until the early 1960s, these performances could be preserved only on kinescope: a grainy, technically imperfect and nonmarketable film shot off a television screen. There was no way to "print up" several hundred copies of a brilliant show and sell it to independent stations, theaters, and foreign markets. In fact, when shows such as *Patterns* were met with acclaim and were repeated, the entire production had to be mounted again from scratch.

Second, the early days of television were marked by far more sponsor control of programming than was the case after the late 1950s. Sponsors had their names on many of the programs (*Alcoa Theatre, The Philco-Goodyear Playhouse, The Kraft Television Theatre*). They were, with few exceptions, hostile to controversy, fearful of it. One reason for the success of the television blacklist was the unsubtle threat of economic retaliation against sponsors of shows using "disloyal" talent. The most famous case involved Laurence Johnson, an upstate New York supermarket owner and prime supporter of Aware, Incorporated, a private investigative group which published *Red Channels* and *Counterattack*, whose lists of "infiltrators" were authoritative to the blacklisters. Johnson threatened uncooperative advertisers with damaging public attack. He promised to display their products in his supermarkets under signs alleging, in effect, that they were manufactured by companies that supported Communist-leaning entertainers. And he vowed to help spread this device to stores outside his control. The threat was often enough to force advertisers into cooperation with the blacklisters. But beyond this, sponsors in the days of early television were fearful that the medium's power was such that any connection between a sponsor and an unpleasantry would poison the mind of the consumer against the sponsor. Erik Barnouw provides endless examples of sponsor interference: a Ford Motor Company functionary ordering the Chrysler Building painted out of the New York City skyline; cigarette manufacturers insisting that all heroes, and no villains, smoke cigarettes in their programs; the American Gas

This 1955 NBC *Producers' Showcase* production starred Henry Fonda, Lauren Bacall (far left), and Humphrey Bogart (back to camera, far right), among others, in a live television version of *Petrified Forest*, Robert E. Sherwood's classic drama.

Frank Sinatra (right) was the Stage Manager and Paul Newman and Eva Marie Saint the principals in this television adaptation of Thornton Wilder's *Our Town*, staged in 1955 for *Producers' Showcase*.

In 1954, *Studio One* presented an original script, Reginald Rose's *Twelve Angry Men*. Taking full advantage of the inherent limits of live studio drama, it was an intense character study of men under pressure, starring Franchot Tone (seated, center), Robert Cummings, Edward Arnold, and Paul Hartman (clustered together, rear center). It later became a successful film starring Henry Fonda and Ed Begley.

Association forcing deletion of the word "gas" in a *Playhouse 90* show, *Judgment at Nuremberg*, thus making it sound as though six million Jews perished in "——— chambers."

A Procter & Gamble memorandum of the 1950s instructed its television time buyers more broadly. "There will," it said, "be no material that may give offense, either directly or by inference, to any commercial organization of any sort . . . There will be no material on any of our programs which could in any way further the concept of business as cold, ruthless, or lacking all sentiment or spiritual motivation."

With live television drama, the sponsor faced a potential battle with a writer and a director every single week. There might be a script about a black family trying to move into the suburbs (changed, under pressure, to an

exconvict); there might be attacks on the criminal justice system, as in *Twelve Angry Men*, or on corporate infighting, as in *Patterns*, or even on television itself, as in *The Velvet Alley*. On live television, an actor might get carried away, as happened one Sunday in a *Philco Playhouse* drama on bigotry, where an actor screamed at a mob, "You goddamn bullies and pigs!" There was, in short, no corporate security.

In fairness, it must be said that advertisers were far from the only fearful purveyors of mass culture in the 1950s. The Hollywood community had been the first to blacklist leftist writers, actors, and directors. Adhering to its own Production Code, Hollywood presented a view of social and sexual conduct that was rampantly dishonest: straying from the path of heterosexual monogamy required divine punishment; married couples slept in twin beds with enough garments to warm an Eskimo; and the makers of a 1953 movie, *The Moon Is Blue,* fought a pitched battle with censors because, among other things, it contained the words "virgin" and "pregnant." Even in the literary world, the cultural climate of the 1950s was very different; for example, the unexpurgated edition of *Lady Chatterley's Lover* could not be legally sold. In the world of movies and books, however, it was—is—always possible for some maverick to break with the prevailing rules, to risk a legal liability, to force the mainstream a bit wider. Should a broadcaster or a sponsor find himself embroiled in controversy, there are a raft of consequences that might follow. A government regulatory agency can remind stations that they exist as federal licensees (for a period in the 1950s, the Federal Communications Commission had a member, John Doerfer, handpicked by Senator Joseph McCarthy); interest groups can pressure sponsors by boycotting their products; sponsors, in turn, could, in the 1950s, pull their advertising from a program, forcing the network to continue it at a loss, or pull it from the schedule. (Today, with sponsors no longer controlling program content or network schedules, such a threat has far less impact.) In a time of uncertainty and fear, corporate advertising—the lifeblood of commercial television—could not accept the sometimes downbeat, sometimes dissenting view of American culture and society presented by many anthology dramas.

There was, however, an even more important element in the decline and fall of original network television drama, one that had its roots in the effort of a junior network to build toward equality with NBC and CBS. NBC was the first broadcasting network, organized in 1926. A year later, United Independent Broadcasters was formed, which soon became CBS. By the 1930s, the two networks were roughly competitive, though it took the "theft" of Jack Benny from NBC in the late 1940s to give CBS its first edge over NBC. (Aptly enough, considering Benny's carefully nurtured image as a miser, CBS won him over by offering him a complex tax-shelter deal to increase his wealth.) But the American Broadcasting Company was a perennial stepchild. It had begun operations with NBC's weaker "blue" network as its foundation in 1943, with virtually no capital, no reputation, no tradition. Its so-called television "network" was virtually nonexistent in the first years of postwar television, and although *The Kraft Television Theatre* split its week between NBC and ABC in 1953 and 1954, the fledgling network had no dramatic offerings of consequence.

Disneyland opened in 1955, a year after Walt Disney began producing a weekly show for ABC, *Disneyland.* Its popularity convinced the other movie studios to go into television production—a move that pulled television west and spelled the end of live, New York–based dramas.

A Supreme Court antitrust ruling in 1948 that movie studios must divest themselves of their theater holdings forced Paramount to split into two companies—Paramount Pictures Corporation and United Paramount Theaters. Looking for a new partner, United Paramount Theaters turned to ABC. In 1953, the merger was completed, and its architect, Leonard Goldenson, took control of the new corporation. By training, by instinct, and in desperation, he turned to Hollywood as a possible source of network programming. While every major studio remained adamantly opposed to producing for television, Goldenson did find his first opening with Walt Disney. In return for the right to plug his movies on the television show and a healthy chunk of ABC investment for his new California amusement park, Disney agreed to supply a weekly show. The *Disneyland* series premiered in 1954 and quickly became the most popular show in the country. More important for the future of television, it convinced the major movie studios that television might be a profitable partner of films instead of its nemesis.

After the success of Walt Disney, Warner Brothers entered the television production field with a series of programs made for the ABC-TV network. Most successful of the first group was *Cheyenne*, starring Clint Walker as frontier scout Cheyenne Bodie.

Another Warner Brothers success: James Garner and Jack Kelly as Bret and Bart Maverick. *Maverick* portrayed an anti-hero, a gambler and a lover rather than a fighter. In one memorable episode entitled "Gunshy," the show parodied *Gunsmoke*.

It was Warner Brothers that broke the ranks of the "majors" by producing for ABC—also in return for the right to plug its films at the end of the shows—a series of filmed adventures called *Warner Bros. Presents*. The series of rotating shows, which began in 1955, included *King's Row, Cheyenne* (the most popular of the first group), and *Colt .45*. Later in the 1950s they offered such successful adventure series as *77 Sunset Strip*. The important thing, however, was that the Hollywood studios began to flock to television as a means of finding work for idle sound stages, cameras, technicians, actors, and producers. And suddenly the full financial dimensions of the filmed series began to strike home. The new product was *film*—it could be run one time or

fifty; it could be rerun with virtually no cost save the projectionist (later the computer operator); it could be sold to independent stations once the network was tired of the show; it could be sold abroad. It was a source of endless profit, as opposed to a one-shot item.

The filmed series had another advantage as well: it was *safe*. Once a show took the form of a regular dramatic series with a continuing set of principal characters, the headache of a weekly battle between writer, producer, director, sponsor, and network was considerably lessened. A network could shape the dimensions of a show even before it went on the air; it could test the concept by showing a pilot to audiences, demographically selected and scientifically monitored, to

An example of television's ability to create appealing characters is found in *77 Sunset Strip*, an early Warner Brothers ABC drama. The ostensible star was Efrem Zimbalist, Jr. *(right)*. But the attention went to Edd Byrnes as the hair-combing "Kookie" (he's shown here with Sue Randall). The character inspired the hit song "Kookie, Kookie, Lend Me Your Comb."

see what characters they liked, what settings excited them. By definition, this was impossible with live, original drama, since an audience could not make a judgment until the show was telecast. Further, live anthology drama had no continuing, sympathetic, attractive character to keep an audience tuned in at the same time every week. This was becoming increasingly important to networks, since, under pressure from the networks, which sought total control over their scheduling, the sponsors were abandoning direct programming. A company might happily sponsor a prestigious show, even if it did not win high ratings, for its own purposes: to project good will, or to reach a select audience. But as the networks took over total control of

choosing the shows that went on the air, it became essential to maximize the audience at every hour of every day, since it was now numbers—not a select time slot—that determined how high the advertising rates went. (For their part, advertisers were finding distinct advantages in scattering their ads across network schedules, instead of risking everything on the hope that an audience might watch its one or two "big" shows.)

The networks were looking for predictability—for the security attending the knowledge that every Tuesday night at 8 P.M. an audience tuned in Milton Berle, or that every Monday night at 9 P.M. *I Love Lucy* appeared. Anthology dramas might light up the numbers one week

In *The Millionaire*, Michael Anthony (played by Marvin Miller) worked for the eccentric billionaire John Beresford Tipton, who dropped a million dollars a week (tax-free) into the laps of unsuspecting folks (here Frank McHugh plays the beneficiary) to see how they would react. The show spawned fantasies the nation over.

A pioneer in writing anthology drama, Rod Serling became disenchanted with television when anthologies died out. He became the host of *Twilight Zone*, a popular fantasy anthology of the early 1960s, and then of *Night Gallery*. Serling was also prominent in commercials. He died of a heart ailment in 1975.

Of course you know who it is. Alfred Hitchcock served as host of his highly popular suspense anthology series.

The Outer Limits, a fantasy anthology of the 1960s, featured the scariest monsters ever seen on television. Here (from left) Jay Novello, Jerry Douglas, Ralph Meeker, and Henry Silva examine an unusual catch.

This champion of regular weekly series featured the brave, stoic hero in constant jeopardy. Marshal Dillon (James Arness, right) spent eighteen years fighting evil, assisted by the gimpy but game Chester (Dennis Weaver) and the hard-boiled but soft-hearted saloon hostess, Kitty (Amanda Blake).

and sag the next. And the costs of those by now antiquated New York studios were becoming impossible. CBS had already begun the move to California in 1956 by telecasting *Playhouse 90* from its new Television City broadcast center—a center built with TV in mind, eliminating the horrendous cost of building, disassembling, transporting, and reassembling sets in New York while dealing with a dozen different craft unions in the process.

So by the late 1950s, Hollywood was the place; the dramatic series was the form; repetition was the key; predictability was the goal. In 1963, with regular weekly anthology dramas all but extinct, and with the series form taking a firm foothold in the network schedules, two Golden Age veterans, Franklin Schaffner, producer-director of *Du Pont Show of the Month*, and Lewis Freedman of *Play of the Week*, recognized basic facts about these dramas that would remain constant over the next fifteen years.

Schaffner talked of "the essential difference between the East Coast and West Coast writer. An East Coast writer comes in, sits down, and says . . . 'I've got an idea.' Then he tells you his story. A West Coast writer comes in, sits down, and says . . . 'What do you want me to write?' "

Freedman noted that "the 'fiction' we talk of has moved away from a conflict of psychology or character, or a conflict of morality, to a conflict of *action*, and that's why we've had the move to film—because film is the best medium for activity. 'Live' TV and the theatre are better suited to a static form in which the action is *interior*."

Schaffner also noted that a viewer accustomed to series drama, with its sudden bursts of action, would find anthology drama increasingly difficult to accept.

"He watches for a minute and a half," he said, "and begins to look at the clock because nobody has been killed yet. No woman is mangled. No child is in terrible danger. Then he rutches around in his seat, and all of a sudden, he's not listening. And if there's any literate quality to the script, he's *got* to be listening."

The American television audience, however, apparently wanted to listen to other fare: to the action-oriented, good-guy-bad-guy format which the Hollywood-produced series presented. They came in fads: *Gunsmoke*, carried over from the successful radio

Wanted—Dead or Alive (top, left), circa 1960, was distinguished primarily by its star, Steve McQueen *(right)*, shown here with Arthur Hunnicut. In *Have Gun—Will Travel (above)*, Richard Boone as Paladin anticipated the James Bond craze with his portrayal of an elegant, sophisticated private agent working for money, not for a government. In *Rawhide (top, right)*, another future movie star, Clint Eastwood *(left, shown with Eric Fleming)*, helped make the West safe for everyone but Indians. *Bat Masterson (right)*, starring Gene Barry *(shown with Adele Mara)*, was a really *different* western. See, he carried a *stick* instead of a gun, and . . .

These famous Hollywood stars were unsuccessful on television. Henry Fonda (*above*; right, shown with Allen Case as Deputy Clay McCord) played Marshall Simon Fry in *The Deputy*, which ran for two years. Fonda also failed as the star of a situation comedy, *The Smith Family*. Tony Curtis, shown here with Brenda Vaccaro, played a lovable con man in *McCoy*, part of *The NBC Sunday Mystery Movie* series. Like Curtis's earlier adventure series, *The Persuaders*, *McCoy* did not last.

drama in 1955, and starring James Arness as the John Wayne–style Marshal Dillon, was for years one of the most popular shows in America. It triggered a spate of western series. By 1959 there were more than thirty regularly scheduled westerns on television every week. In that year, all of the top three shows and five of the top ten were westerns. "You know what differentiated them?" former CBS programming chief Mike Dann once recalled. "The size of the *gun*. Steve McQueen [in *Wanted: Dead or Alive*] had a sawed-off shotgun. Chuck Connors [*The Rifleman*] had a rifle. Paladin [protagonist of *Have Gun—Will Travel*] put a revolver in a holster with a chess knight on it."

The fads and trends kept changing. There were "quirky cop" fads—law enforcement types with odd foibles. Cannon was fat; Longstreet was blind; Columbo was outwardly sloppy; Barnaby Jones was a "countrified Columbo," according to his creator. There were "empire westerns" featuring tightly knit families of dynastic scope. *Bonanza* triggered that fad; *The High Chaparral*, *The Virginian*, and others followed suit. There were repeated cycles of doctor shows, from the

A western motif for the spy fad of the mid-1960s was employed in *Wild, Wild West*. Robert Conrad and Ross Martin (behind bars, right) played secret agents for President Grant. Here they are prisoners of the notorious Dr. Lovelace, played by Michael Dunn (foreground), supported by Phoebe Dorin.

Ironside (left) and *Columbo* provide two examples of "humanized" police officers. San Francisco police chief Ironside, played by Raymond Burr, was crippled by a sniper's bullet and confined to a wheelchair. (Burr is shown here with loyal aides played by Don Galloway, behind Burr, and Don Mitchell. Elizabeth Baur is at far left.) Columbo, portrayed fetchingly by Peter Falk, is a sloppy, blood-fearing cop with a working-class background who undoes the (always) wealthy, powerful criminal.

James Drury (left, shown here with Sara Lane and Don Quine), starred in *The Virginian*. This NBC western was the first regular series to break the one-hour convention and appear as a long-form (ninety-minute) drama.

Bonanza—the ultimate family western. Lorne Greene (center) reigned as Ben Cartwright, patriarch of the Ponderosa Ranch (roughly the size of western Europe), shown here with his sons Hoss (Dan Blocker, left) and Little Joe (Michael Landon). So tightly knit was this family that the threat of the family being separated by a son's romance had to be met by divine intervention: the girl died.

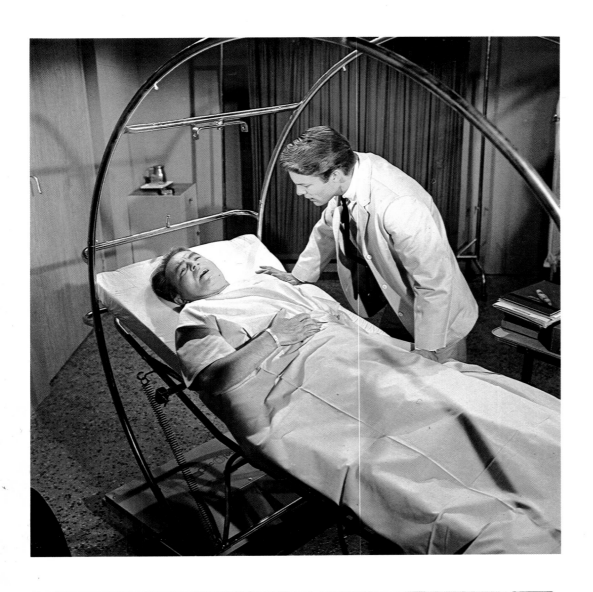

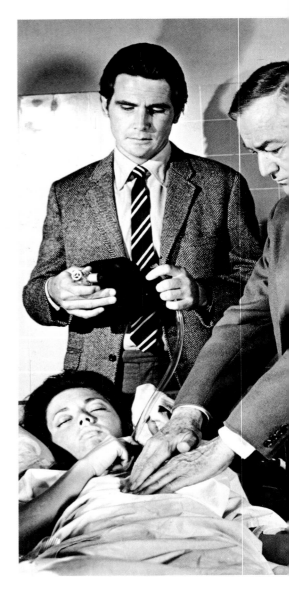

Because doctors hold the power of life and death in their hands, they are natural heroes dramatic series. In *Dr. Kildare* (above, left), Richard Chamberlain was the idealistic youn intern in a series adapted from the movie hits Chad Everett as Joe Gannon on *Medical Cer (left)* found that personal and emotional crise inevitably accompanied the physical problem of patients who came into his care. On *Marcu Welby, M.D. (above)*, Robert Young and Jam Brolin (here attending JoAnn Pflug) not only made house calls; they also drove patients home, did a little light housework, and never seemed to present a bill.

Lawyers, like doctors, are credible series heroes because they work with people whose lives are in crisis. In *Perry Mason (left)*, Raymond Burr bested D.A. Hamilton Burger (William Talman) week after week—with this one exception—by inducing dramatic courtroom confessions. An exceptional series was *The Defenders*, which aired on CBS in the early sixties. It featured a father-and-son team played by E. G. Marshall (at bench in middle) and Robert Reed (seated, right), who took on highly sensitive issues—censorship, capital punishment, blacklisting, abortion. Here they oppose J. D. Cannon (left), who later appeared as a harassed police captain on *McCloud*.

early *Medic* to *Ben Casey* and *Doctor Kildare* to *Marcus Welby, M.D.* and *Medical Center*. There were endless lawyer shows. Raymond Burr as *Perry Mason* was the most durable; Reginald Rose's *The Defenders*, starring E. G. Marshall and Robert Reed, was the most distinguished. There were old, crusty, but lovable cops teamed with young, idealistic, naïve, but lovable cops; old, crusty, but lovable doctors teamed with young, idealistic, naïve, but lovable doctors.

But beyond the names and trends are the characteristics that defined the overwhelming majority of these shows, and so severely limited them in their dramatic range. First, the shows required audience empathy with the principal. In his master's thesis, a young graduate student noted of ABC's action shows of the late 1950s that "each . . . has a leading man with whom the audience can easily identify. They are all distinct personalities—flesh and blood characters who possess an intangible quality which makes them real and believable." (This student, named Fred Silverman, became the head of CBS programming at the age of thirty-two. Five years later, he became the programming chief of ABC and pulled it into prime-time dominance for the first time in the network's history.) The search for audience em-

A bright lad, a brighter dog, danger, rescue; it's been sure-fire for forty years. In this episode of *Lassie*, Jan Clayton reads a note as Tommy Rettig looks on. Lassie corrects the spelling.

Lloyd Bridges was frequently all wet and so were many of the plots, but *Sea Hunt* contained exceptional underwater photography.

In a classic dramatic formula, two attractive young men (George Maharis, left, and Martin Milner) travel around the country in their Corvette, finding action, adventure, and romance. *Route 66* provided a mix of escape, involvement, and freedom that appealed to the homebound viewer.

pathy helps explain the producers' and programmers' ceaseless search for some kind of "humanizing" quality to offset the totally predictable nature of the plots faced by the hero. If Raymond Burr is to play a tough police chief in *Ironside*, make him a cripple in a wheelchair to give him a touch of humanity. If Telly Savalas must play a tough police chief battling the dregs of New York underworld life in *Kojak*, then make the audience sit up and take notice of his habit of sucking lollipops—a childlike quirk for such a tough man. Even when a character is required to *not* express emotion—as Matt Dillon was in *Gunsmoke*—he should be surrounded by colorful, "quirky" friends—as Matt Dillon was, with the limping, faithful Chester (Dennis Weaver), the hard-boiled but engaging Kitty (Amanda Blake), the crusty, folk-wise Doc (Milburn Stone).

Second, these characters *must* be involved in a larger-than-life enterprise, one that places life-or-death questions in their hands, if not subjecting them to life-or-death danger, every week. Michael Eisner, who used to run West Coast programming operations for ABC and then became head of television production with Paramount, explains that "it's very difficult to find twenty-four stories to spend an hour with that aren't in-

Star Trek, which aired on NBC for 3 years and was saved from cancellation in 1967–68 by one of the largest outpourings of viewer mail in television history, still has a large, passionate following. The crew of the starship U.S.S. *Enterprise* (Leonard Nimoy, William Shatner, and DeForest Kelley, from left) was aided by occasional scripts of the highest science-fiction caliber. Gene Roddenberry was the creator and executive producer of the show.

One good reason for so many police shows is that they can plausibly deal with a wide range of problems, from the violent to the social. And, as certified "tough guys," policemen can also become involved with each other without raising eyebrows. A very successful combination of police drama and male-bonding was NBC's *Adam-12*, starring Kent McCord and Martin Milner (right). They are shown here aiding a homeless young mother (Jenny Sullivan) and her daughter.

Paul Michael Glaser (as Starsky, left) and David Soul play the leads in *Starsky and Hutch*, a typical dramatic formula show. They are good buddies, they make their own rules, they drive a distinctive car, they shoot guns, they save each other's lives, they chase bad guys very fast in their distinctive car, they get hurt, they don't die, they always get their man . . .

volved with life or death. How do you do a show about an accountant or a steelworker week in and week out?" Fred Silverman, when asked why the close friends in series such as *Starsky and Hutch* always seemed to be policemen or doctors, exclaimed, "What are they going to be? Architects? What will happen to them?" The same network's research chief, Marvin Mord, observed that "once you have a character the audience cares about, and once you place that character in a life-jeopardizing situation, the audience is involved." And real situations? "You wouldn't watch it. People are not willing to accept real problems in television drama. A program that attempts to deal with the harsh realities of life tends to turn viewers off."

This attitude is by no means confined to any one net-

work. Perry Lafferty, for many years a top CBS programmer, once observed that he and his fellow programmers "couldn't think of a continuing hour show in which the hero didn't have the power of life and death—you have to give him a gun or a scalpel or a lawbook, and a jeopardy situation."

To one practitioner, that "jeopardy" is a matter of strict form. Quinn Martin, who produced *The Untouchables* and who heads the company that produces *The Streets of San Francisco, Cannon, Barnaby Jones, Most Wanted*, and other melodramas, explains: "It's a classic form: opening action, the middle jeopardy, and end action. You *need* the middle jeopardy to get the audience back after the minute-forty-five [commercial break]. If you don't have jeopardy in the middle break, they'll

A genuine break with dramatic formulas came with *The Waltons (left)*. The large clan struggled through the Depression but never abandoned its familial ties. The family included Michael Learned as the mother (bottom left) and Will Geer as Grandpa (at the head of the table). At his right sits Richard Thomas as John-Boy; at his left is Ellen Corby as Grandma. NBC followed much the same formula with *Little House on the Prairie*, adapted from the novels of Laura Ingalls Wilder. Michael Landon, Karen Grassie (as the parents), Melissa Gilbert (as Laura, top), Melissa Sue Anderson, and Lindsay and Sidney Greenbush (who alternate as baby Carrie) played the family struggling through pioneer life.

switch the channel. You have to have something so they'll say, 'Jesus, I want to see what's going to happen.'" (In soap opera, this heightened tension before the commercial is known as "the consternation fadeout.")

Third, jeopardy often implies some connection with violence, or, as networks prefer to describe it, "action-adventure." This issue has obsessed students of television since its inception. By 1950, studies were already underway on the effect of televised violence on children, and the U.S. Surgeon General's report of 1972 did find what it described as a "modest" causal link between televised violence and aggressive patterns of behavior. But, in fact, except for some notorious examples—*The Untouchables*, whose treatment of or-

ganized crime in the 1920s is surely the most violent television series in history, and a *Bus Stop* episode, "Told by an Idiot," featuring singer Fabian as a sadistic killer—the issue is not really violence at all. The essential element is a situation sufficiently tense and anxious to put the series' principal character in an atmosphere of danger, sufficiently simplistic to be resolved in fifty-two minutes. In the spring of 1975, the three networks, acting in what was later found to be unconstitutional collusion with the FCC, promulgated a "family hour." They moved sex and violence out of the early prime-time period and generally toned down killings. What happened was that the shows featured violent treatment of *objects* instead of people. The "main titles" (the opening credits) of *Starsky and Hutch*, the biggest new "ac-

Ralph Bellamy played Mike Barnett in *The Man Against Crime (left)*, one of the first (1949) action dramas; it was telecast live from the CBS Grand Central Station studios. One of the least-remembered adventure shows was *Johnny Staccato*, presented by NBC in 1959 to 1960. It starred John Cassavetes, who fought crime in his spare time. His job? Modern jazz pianist.

Richard Carlson played Herbert Philbrick, c terspy against domestic Communism, in thi Cold War action drama, *I Led Three Lives*.

◄ One of the most popular syndicated shows (distributed not by a network, but by ZIV, an independent production company) starred Broderick Crawford (left) in *Highway Patrol*. This show, which began in 1956, concerned crime fighting but preached traffic safety as well, and made the police radio code "ten-four" a national catchphrase.

The Untouchables began on CBS as a two-part, two-hour drama in 1959, then moved to ABC where it gained enormous ratings and a reputation as perhaps the most violent show in television history. Robert Stack played Eliot Ness, head of the incorruptible Federal Special Squad known as the Untouchables during Prohibition. Neville Brand played Al Capone. The series was narrated by Walter Winchell and produced for Desilu Studios by Quinn Martin. He later became the head of his own production company and a major supplier of action-adventure shows.

ack Webb (left) was creator and star of Dragnet, one of e first and best police-action shows. As Det. Sgt. Friday f the Los Angeles Police Department, Webb played taut, clipped, policeman who wanted "just the facts, a'am." Ben Alexander played his partner, Officer Smith. ragnet was noteworthy for the character vignettes in-erted between the action and for its compelling, memora-le musical theme.

If drama involves in part the willing suspension of disbelief, then Mission: Impossible, a CBS hit series produced by Bruce Geller, set all kinds of dramatic records. (top): Steven Hill (second from right) starred as the head of a remarkably talented team of spies (from left, Greg Morris, Barbara Bain, Martin Landau, and Peter Lupus) who weekly penetrated the security strongholds of sinister dictatorships by speaking heavily accented English and wearing uniforms. They never simply killed off their enemies; instead, they staged mock nuclear attacks and other electronic diversions to defeat evil. (above): Peter Graves later assumed the role of chief commando.

◄ Mannix was a typical detective show, starring Mike Connors as a private eye, Gail Fisher as his secretary, and a patterned sport jacket playing itself. Car chases, gun duels, life-and-death jeopardy every week . . .

One of the longest-running cop shows is CBS's *Hawaii Five-O*, starring Jack Lord. Although the show's scenery is its chief distinguishing characteristic, in 1977, after nine years, it was still on the air.

Robert Blake is the special asset of *Baretta*, an ABC detective show. He turns in what may well be the best acting on any regular series as the lead; in Blake's hands, the conventional cop-who-breaks-the-rules-but-gets-the-villain-and-cares-about-people format is credible.

tion" hit of the first Family Hour season, featured the classic car-chase screeching-tires montage with the two heroes running down villains, pursuing their foe—and concluding with a huge automobile explosion. Whatever can keep the audience concerned with the plight of the hero or heroine will suffice.

To many of the most successful members of the television industry, the all-but-exclusive franchise of the series in regularly scheduled television drama was what one could expect of a mass medium. Frank Price, president of Universal Television, the biggest supplier of prime-time network programming for many years, notes that "in essence, TV has replaced the *Saturday Evening Post*, the slicks, hard-covered books, and radio. We have taken commercial fiction over." Universal, to be sure, has had its share of casualties in this world of rigid commercial-fiction rules. In one season, it supplied two series that attempted to bend these rules—*Sunshine*, about a young widower of the sixties generation and his daughter, and *The Law*, a worm's-eye view of the criminal justice system. Both survived only a short time on NBC.

What concerns others, including Frank Price and other successful people in the television industry, is that the rigid forms of these series never permit anything to happen to a character that might remotely be con-

NBC's *Police Woman*, starring Angie Dickinson as Suzanne "Pepper" Anderson, added an audience-grabbing twist to the familiar police melodrama script. In a remarkably high percentage of assignments, Pepper is required to appear in skimpy, revealing clothes.

The biggest hit of the 1976–77 season, and something of a national phenomenon, *Charlie's Angels* starred (from right) Farrah Fawcett-Majors, Kate Jackson, and Jaclyn Smith as three employees of a detective agency. The plots were unimportant. The tight clothing, the lack of underwear, the bikinis, and the cheerful sexploitation of the three attractive women made the show—and Farrah in particular—a permanent feature of tabloids and magazines.

Combining a law enforcement motif (he's an agent for a CIA-like American government division) and a comic-book super-hero element (he's got bionic strength and vision) made *The Six Million Dollar Man* a high-rated Sunday night show on ABC. Lee Majors (also known as Farrah Fawcett-Majors's husband) played Steve Austin (left) and Richard Anderson played his boss, Oscar Goldman.

The only recent successful anthology drama, NBC's *Police Story*, offers unusually realistic portrayals of the tensions and complexities in the lives of police officers. Here, Don Meredith (right) and David Groh (better known as Rhoda Morgenstern's ex-husband) appear in a 1976 episode.

nected with reality. Almost fifteen years ago, Paul Monash, who developed *Peyton Place* for television as an early "nighttime soap opera," said of the series form that "your hero is a repetitious man who does not develop, in terms of himself, over the course of thirty hours a year." (As the cost of television shows increased, networks gradually reduced the number of original episodes from thirty-nine to twenty-two per season, beginning reruns in March.) *Police Story* executive producer Stanley Kallis made the same point more than a decade later. A dramatic lead, he said, "is a function, not a human being. He's not gonna die, he's not gonna quit his job, he's not gonna grow in dimension. So the

writer starts off with a leading character who's not interesting. You have to find meaningful problems for him to deal with. So each week, you give him a surrogate problem."

This kind of show, however well done it may be, however entertaining it may be—and some of them, such as *Kojak, N.Y.P.D.*, the early *Dragnet*, contained first-rate writing and acting—violates one of the essential precepts of drama: that the protagonist goes through a crisis from which he emerges changed. The essence of the series is that there be no *real* threat. Audiences, some television executives argue, don't *want* ambiguity. "Defeat and dreariness are what happens to

George C. Scott played social worker Neil Brock in *East Side/West Side,* a Talent Associates drama that many consider one of the finest regular series ever shown on commercial television. Here were poverty, unhappy endings, frustration—small triumphs and losses instead of the routine, ultimately trivial victories of the good guys on an assembly-line basis.

A television tour de force: Art Carney as an alcoholic in a one-hour, one-character drama, *Call Me Back,* shown on NBC in 1960.

you during the day," says ABC vice-president, Bob Shanks, in his book *The Cool Fire*. "At night, in front of the box, most people want to share in victories, associate with winners, be transported from reality." Every regular television watcher, including reasonably bright four-year-old children, knows that the protagonist will come out of every scrape in more or less the same shape he went into it, if for no other reason than because if Kojak gets shot, there's no more series.

Two of the best regular series to appear on network television were *The Defenders*, starring E. G. Marshall, and *East Side/West Side*, starring George C. Scott. Both shows had dared to go beyond the formula, not just by dealing with such controversial issues as abortion, capital punishment, residential integration, and even blacklisting, but by suggesting that not every dilemma ended happily. In the early 1960s, Marshall and Scott discussed whether their characters could develop over a period of time. Scott suggested that "if the classic idea of resolution is the goal, then at the end of some forecasted period, there should be some true resolution of the central character. There can be change in this sense. Some day, Brock [the social worker played by Scott] will face this—death, total resignation, incapacity . . . but not every week . . . We are really talking about the longest drama in history."

Indeed, in the last show of the series, Brock was given the opportunity to become a top aide to a charismatic political figure whose goal was the presidency of the United States. By implication, the end of the show was itself strong evidence that he did in fact take the job.

This premise, however, was anathema to the very idea of the continuing series and unthinkable in view of the commercial possibilities of a long-running dramatic show. By the 1960s, the networks had adopted a pattern called "deficit financing" of series. Put bluntly, this meant that the license fees paid to suppliers of shows (the money paid by a network for the right to run a show) did not pay the costs of producing that show. A series that ran for one or two years and was then canceled actually ended up costing the production company a fortune. The road to profit lay in keeping a show on the network long enough to accumulate a package of shows which could then be sold to independent stations and foreign markets for enormous profits. The concept of a continuing story was all but inconceivable to networks, apart from the daytime soap-opera form. In fact, when in the early 1960s Paul Monash suggested a

Lee J. Cobb and Mildred Dunnock starred in Arthur Miller's *Death of a Sales man*, shown on CBS in 1966. This study of an ordinary man's tragedy, with focus on character, was uniquely suited to the television screen; it was a r minder of what television had left behin

In *Missiles of October*, an example of the "docu-drama"—the fictional portrayal of a real event—Nehemiah Persoff and Howard DaSilva as Soviet leaders Andrei Gromyko and Nikita Khrushchev *(left)* confront William Devane as President John Kennedy (shown here with James Callahan as Kennedy aide Dave Powers) over the Cuban missile crisis.

CBS broadcast *Fear on Trial* in 1975, a fictionalized version of John Henry Faulk's attempt to fight the political blacklist of the 1950s—in this case, a blacklist whose collaborators had included CBS. George C. Scott (left) played defense attorney Louis Nizer, and William Devane (front, center) played Faulk.

An ABC made-for-TV movie that was at sharp variance with the Indian stereotypes of early television westerns was *I Will Fight No More, Forever*, which was broadcast in April, 1975. Here, Ned Romero as Chief Joseph and Linda Redfern as his wife are shown.

Dennis Weaver played a Taos, New Mexico, law enforcement officer who brought his rural ways to New York in *McCloud*. This drama, from ninety minutes to two hours long, is one of the rotating series with the overall title *The NBC Sunday Mystery Movie*.

The made-for-TV movie frequently deals with themes considered too sensational or explicit for regular series fare. NBC's *A Case of Rape (left)* starred Elizabeth Montgomery as the victim of both a rapist and official callousness. CBS's *Helter Skelter*, a two-part dramatization of the story of the Tate-LaBianca murders by the Charles Manson clan, was a ratings smash.

One of the most popular movies of all time, *Gone with the Wind*, drew one of the largest audiences in television history when it was broadcast in two parts on NBC in the fall of 1976.

Cicely Tyson won critical acclaim and a large audience with her portrayal of a 110-year-old ex-slave in a 1974 CBS special, *The Autobiography of Miss Jane Pittman*. Here she challenges racial segregation by drinking at a "white-only" water fountain.

The long-running saga of the Bellamy family and their ▶ loyal core of servants, *Upstairs Downstairs*, originally shown on British television, won a devoted American following, especially among people who would never admit to enjoying soap opera. The Bellamy family ("Upstairs"; *top*) included (from left) Lesley-Anne Down, David Langton, and Simon Williams, served by Gordon Jackson. The servants ("Downstairs") were played by (from left) Angela Baddeley, Christopher Beeny, Gordon Jackson, Jacqueline Tong, and Jenny Tomasin. Jean Marsh (not shown), who played Rose, was one of the program's creators.

"novelistic" show, taking the characters of Irwin Shaw's *The Young Lions* and following them through the post–World War II years, programmers thought he was talking about a typical series such as *Combat* or *The Gallant Men*.

Instead, the network alternatives to the dramatic series, apart from the increasingly rare special offerings of *The Hallmark Hall of Fame*, and the short-lived *ABC Stage '67* and *CBS Playhouse*, were made-for-TV movies and the "long-form" (more than one-hour long) shows. The movies, pioneered by the perennially series-short ABC, did provide alternatives to the limited categories of dramatic series. Characters *could* pass through crises, even die, as did the star of the Chicago Bears, Brian Piccolo, in the story of his battle with cancer, *Brian's Song*. Delicate themes could be dealt with, including homosexuality, as in *That Certain Summer*. In the early 1970s, the networks began to present fictional portrayals of real-life events. These so-called "docu-dramas" explored, among other things, the Pueblo incident, the Cuban missile crisis, even—in *Fear on Trial*—television blacklisting of the 1950s.

NBC had begun programming long-form shows, first with *The Virginian*, and then with a number of ninety-minute- or two-hour-long shows with revolving characters, including *The Bold Ones* and *NBC Mystery Movie*. These helped relieve the more confining limits of the

regular series. In essence, however, these two alternatives were minor bends in a narrow stream of programming possibilities. The made-for-TV movies, for example, often exploited genres that rarely survived in a regular series, such as fantasy and horror.

By the early 1970s, as Mercury Theatre veteran John Houseman wrote, original television drama was virtually a thing of the past on commercial television. More than half of the original network dramas were presented on public television, and half of those were imported from British television. Network drama was the province of artificial heroes struggling against artificial dilemmas, of no real relevance to the viewers, and always conquering them. Most of these heroes were without family, children, communities, distant from friends, neighbors, roots.

Ironically, it was one of those British imports that provided the first step toward what was to become a potentially significant alternative to the weekly, repetitive series. In 1969–1970, the Public Broadcasting System presented *The Forsyte Saga*—an adaptation of John Galsworthy's novels—in which characters grew, changed, even died. The response of the television industry was at first skeptical. Said David Victor, creator and executive producer of the *Marcus Welby, M.D.* series, "there was no follow-up for the next season. The secret of a good series is that you must be able to see

162

Peter Strauss and Susan Blakeley were two of the lead characters in the ABC "mini-series" adapted from Irwin Shaw's novel about two brothers in postwar America, *Rich Man, Poor Man*. The 1976 mini-series killed off one brother, Tom Jordache; the less successful weekly series the following year (*Rich Man, Poor Man—Book II*) ended by killing off Strauss's character, Rudy Jordache. This willingness to dispose of popular characters was a sharp break with conventional television tradition. Oh yes, Blakeley's character was killed off early in *Book II*.

episode thirty-five or forty-nine before you begin." But the reception to *The Forsyte Saga*, and, later, to London Weekend Television's *Upstairs Downstairs*, did trigger the interest of the commercial networks.

In 1975, CBS attempted to emulate the success of *Upstairs Downstairs* with its American version, *Beacon Hill*. Set in Boston of the post–World War I era, the story of the wealthy Lassiter family failed in the ratings. But the following spring, ABC scored a huge ratings hit with a "novel for television," a twelve-hour version of Irwin Shaw's *Rich Man, Poor Man*. Granted, the "mini-series," as it was known, had more than its share of commercial attractions, including a generous dose of sex and violence. But it also featured a continuing story in which the principal characters exhibited both positive and negative qualities. In the last episode of the presentation, one of the two leading characters was killed. If it was something less than high art, it was something more than the cookie-cutter that network drama had become.

In the following season, the mini-series became a regular alternative on network television. NBC adapted a series of novels, each running six or seven weeks. And ABC's adaptation of Alex Haley's book, *Roots*,

The most popular show in American television history, ABC's *Roots*, was telecast in January, 1977, on eight consecutive nights. The twelve-hour version of author Alex Haley's search for his family's African origins and slave past—a blend of fact and fiction—captured more than half of the American population at some point in its run. Here Cicely Tyson as Binta admires the new-born Kunta Kinte, who will be sold into slavery as a young man. Maya Angelou looks on.

presented on eight consecutive nights, captured the American television audience as no other programming experiment had ever done. When the series ended, *Roots* had become the most watched program of all time.

These "mini-series," it must be said, do no violence to Universal Television President Price's notion that network television is engaged in "commercial fiction." They are works made for the action-oriented Hollywood touch; they are packages that leave little room for the kind of original, small-scale, probing dramas of the early age of television. But given the economics of the increasingly profitable and increasingly competitive networks, given their ceaseless search for products that can lure the audience away from the other networks, these mini-series are at least a step away from the most rigid of molds in which network drama has trapped itself over the last decade and a half.

ADVERTISING

The Selling
of America

Every advertising medium uses familiar personalities to help the customer form the proper image of the product. The Mercury automobile wants to cultivate a sense of glamour and wealth; its symbol is movie star Catherine Deneuve *(below)*. Comet cleanser wants to achieve a sense of unfancy, just-plain-folks competence. Its symbol: former movie star Jane Withers *(right)* as "Josephine the Plumber." To demonstrate trustworthiness and reliability, Henry Fonda *(left)* appears for GAF cameras and other GAF products.

To many of television's critics, advertising is the symbol of all that is wrong with the medium. The commercials, they say, are intrusive, repetitious, and dishonest, and appeal to the viewers' base, material instincts. They turn a communications medium of unparalleled power into a vast wasteland, a Turkish bazaar, a patent-medicine show. Their exaggerations, their sometimes crude cajoling by fantasy and hyperbole have made commercials the targets of outrage and satire from the early days of Milton Berle to the contemporary assaults of Carol Burnett and *Saturday Night*.

The facts suggest a different reading. Advertisers use television the way they have used every mass medium from the first days of widespread newspaper circulation. They have discovered that television lends itself to certain techniques of selling which are especially powerful because the medium is powerful. The unique contribution of television to advertising is its prodigious ability to communicate not simply information about a product, but also fantasies about consumers and how they choose to live. Because advertising is, after all, the *raison d'être* of commercial television, commercials are more carefully prepared, more elaborately produced, and more frequently seen than any one program on television. The combined impact of these messages produces an almost atmospheric presence of commercial messages. To listen to a two-year-old child flawlessly recite a cereal slogan is to understand clearly the power of televised salesmanship. The fundamental fact, however, is that it is the decision to finance and operate television for maximum profits, supplied totally by advertising, that

Major information was conveyed visually in two famous advertising campaigns. To demonstrate that Timex *(below)* has a durable product, its watches were put through the tortures of the damned; here a watch is strapped to the wrist of a water-skier in this 1966 commercial. To remind viewers of the fragility of expensive automobiles, State Farm uses the most familiar symbol of fragility: the egg.

It's slow good.

Television advertising combines the techniques of every other available medium. This Heinz ketchup ad includes modern graphics, a dramatic visual illustration of the theme ("It's slow good") and a few seconds from Carly Simon's song "Anticipation."

has turned the medium into a marketplace. Blaming advertisers for using a tool of unequaled reach, range, and intimacy to blare their messages is like blaming an insurance salesman for opening his briefcase after you have invited him into your home and expressed concern for your family's financial security.

Every new method of reaching potential customers occasions a new technique of advertising. The newspapers of the seventeenth century were filled with promises that teeth cleaners would make teeth "white as ivory" while sweetening the breath and holding loose teeth fast. In the eighteenth century, advertisements hawked the healthful effects of tobacco to cure poor eyesight and flagging sexual energies. (Wrote Samuel Johnson, "Promise, large promise, is the soul of advertising.") In nineteenth-century America, the national postal network enabled Montgomery Ward & Company and Sears Roebuck and Company to establish a national marketing pattern through the use of enormous catalogues offering infinitely more than any local store. The arrival of those catalogues in small American towns was an event of major importance each year, equal in ritual significance to the first harbinger of spring. And with the rise of national magazines in the first two decades of the twentieth century, national brand advertising became possible. Such companies as the American Tobacco Company, the National Biscuit Company (Nabisco), and the major

Adventure in patronage: *(top)* smoke a small Scandinavian cigar, and somehow you are in the middle of New York harbor on a Viking ship. Invest in the Dreyfus Fund *(above)* and be confident in the knowledge that your company is a veritable lion— king of the Wall Street jungle.

auto companies flourished in part because they had the reach and the advertising power to override any number of local or regional companies.

Broadcasting was simply an innovative way to bring an advertising message directly into the home. The fact that it employed the spoken word made for different tactics—to take an obvious example, it made the singing commercial, the jingle, an American phenomenon. The social message of radio advertising, however, was linked closely to the social message of advertising in the mass magazines. As advertising executive Joseph Seldin wrote, the advertiser in the 1920s was "learning to pay less attention to the special qualities and advantages of his product, and more to the study of what [people] wanted: to be young and desireable, to be rich, to keep up with the Joneses, to be envied." In an era when the magazines were running endless messages warning of "B.O." (body odor), pink toothbrush, and conspicuous nose pores— Listerine presented weekly full-page stories of lives ruined forever because of bad breath or other, more intimate, olfactory offenses—broadcast advertising was part of a general movement toward exploiting the social fears of the American consumer.

Those who had built the industry did not intend broadcasting to become a commercial vehicle. In the 1920s, everyone from Secretary of Commerce Herbert Hoover to the broadcasters themselves, including RCA executive David Sarnoff, were firmly opposed to paid commercial messages. The advertising community, however, discovered radio to be a much stronger selling force than any they had known. They could not rest with the limited right to have a sponsor's name mentioned as a patron of a program—much as public television mentions the name of a funding company today. Under the leadership of such advertising giants as Albert Lasker of Lord & Thomas, sponsors won the right to broadcast commercial messages in return for sponsoring programs. Indeed, as network radio grew, sponsors actually bought blocks of time on a network—Pepsodent weeknights at 7 P.M. for *Amos 'n' Andy*, Jell-O on Sunday nights for Jack Benny—and developed the programs themselves.

By the time network television became a reality in the late 1940s, the structural pattern of financing programs was firmly entrenched. Milton Berle's show was actually *The Texaco Star Theatre*, with service-station attendants opening the show ("Tonight we may be showmen, but . . . tomorrow we'll be servicing your car!"). Sponsors were clearly identified with specific

In television's early days, when sponsors packaged and paid for programming by themselves, advertisers found many ways to increase the frequency of their messages. Here *Ted Mack and the Original Amateur Hour (top)* offers viewers a permanent reminder of the advertiser. Similarly, *Beat the Clock (center),* with host Bud Collyer, utilized the clock as a billboard for Hazel Bishop, one of the first cosmetics companies to use television advertising to the hilt. On *What's My Line?* (*bottom*; moderator John Daly watches mystery guest Carmen Miranda sign in), the Stopette deodorant was as prominent as panelists Dorothy Kilgallen, Bennett Cerf, and Arlene Francis (the fourth panelist was a guest; here it's writer Hal Block).

One of the first examples of exploiting television's possibilities was this inventive 1949 campaign showing Lucky Strike cigarettes marching and square dancing across the screen. Frame-by-frame filming of stop-action sequences gave the cigarettes the appearance of animation.

Animation, never before possible in mass advertising, came into its own with television. Sports fans watched Gillette's Cavalcade of Sports throughout television's early years (Gillette sponsored the World Series and the Friday night fights, among other events), and with those events came a parrot *(above)* asking "How Are Ya Fixed for Blades?" Ajax cleanser *(below)* employed animated elfs to sing "Use Ajax, the foaming cleanser/Cleans the dirt/right down the drain."

programs: *Voice of Firestone, The Bell Telephone Hour, The Kraft Television Theatre, The United States Steel Hour.* It was, in effect, a holdover from the earliest days of radio, when sponsors hoped in part to earn the gratitude of listeners in return for paying for programming.

The advertisers in the early days of television were, like the early programs, fascinated with the sheer magic of being able to *show* something to the viewer. Lucky Strike cigarettes jumped out of the pack, square danced, did close-order drills; pitchmen on local stations were given thirty minutes to extol the virtues of lanolin through history, ending in a pitch for Charles Antell Formula #5. (It was the beginning of the Alberto-Culver empire, a packaging concern built wholly through television advertising.) Other pitchmen showed us miraculously easy-to-use storm and screen windows and Chop-a-Matic kitchen aids which turned potatoes into complex geometrical shapes at the flick of a wrist.

Sometimes it was enough to simply show a product on a popular show. Hazel Bishop lipstick, an aggressive advertiser in the first few years of television (*This Is Your Life*), carved out a powerful hold on the market, only to lose much of that market when Revlon began sponsoring *The $64,000 Question* in 1955. Its popularity literally caused a run on Revlon's lipstick. And the impact of the medium was so strong that it could make celebrities of announcers. Betty Furness, a model who opened and closed Westinghouse refrigerator doors at the 1952 national nominating conventions, became a nationally known figure in a matter of days.

In these early years, sponsors and advertising agencies were chiefly responsible for the packaging of television programs. And with that responsibility came frequent intrusions into the content of those programs. Apart from their repeated battles with writers and producers over dramatic material, and apart from their capitulation to the blacklist, sponsors often exercised more blatantly unethical controls. When the quiz show scandals erupted in the late 1950s, grand juries and congressional committees heard testimony that the advertisers had had a heavy hand in the rigging of the shows, demanding that more "attractive" contestants keep winning in order to involve the audiences and boost the ratings. Partly as a consequence of these revelations, and partly because the networks were coming to realize how powerful they were, the networks absorbed virtually all control over the choosing and scheduling of network programs by the end of the 1950s.

Rex Marshall was one of the first and most enduring of television's pitchmen; note here the relatively primitive use of graphics and the slight visual impact.

Subtlety was not the strong point of Gunilla Knutson's appeal to men in this 1966 Noxzema shave cream campaign; the accompanying music was "The Stripper" as Gunilla coaxed men to: "Take it off . . . take it *all* off."

As television developed, advertisers began to understand that the visual possibilities of the medium made the link between products and life-styles easier to devise than ever before. Ads did not have to *promise* a better sex life or richer life-style; they could depict it right before the customer's eyes. The 1950s saw kitchen products and floor waxes set in fifteen-thousand-dollar kitchens; the 1960s saw the youth culture exploited in brilliant soft-drink advertising. With explosions of colors, scenes of young people in exuberant play, and rapid cutting of film, these ads capitalized on the TV generation's impatience with "talking heads"—people conversing on the television without visually arresting support—and its craving for instant gratification. In fact, the visual power of television enabled advertisers to sell, along with their products, not-so-subtle messages about social values.

These underlying messages, for example, would shore up consumers who might be feeling guilty at the freedom new products were promising them. If mothers were vaguely uneasy about fast, frozen convenience foods, they were assured that "nothing says loving like something from the oven, and Pillsbury says it best." If they felt guilty serving an artificial lemonade mix, Wyler's would show them a down-home Ma and Pa Kettle couple, complete with gingham dress for Ma and overalls for Pa, enjoying a glass. Morningstar Farms, trying to sell "sausages" made from textured vegetable protein, packaged its product with a bucolic farm scene, called itself "Morningstar *Farms*," and featured television advertising with a big Sunday country breakfast. For its egg substitute, an ad with an animated egg was shown. By the 1970s, the same convenience food that made mothers of the 1950s feel guilty made a more positive pitch to assertive, career-minded women, this time promising them more time to fulfill personal aspirations.

And, in the late 1960s and early 1970s, sensing that Americans were concerned with a loss of roots and yearned for a simpler way of life, advertising linked their products with that simpler way of life by association. A whole series of ads on television—for Coca-Cola, for Kodak, for Chevrolet, for foods of all sorts— were set in old, rambling country homes, with huge family reunions around enormous picnic tables. "Let Country Morning take you back again," coaxed one breakfast cereal. In an allied campaign, RC cola showed young people disenchanted with big-city life turning to another way of existence: motorcycling across the country; coming home to Nashville from a

(This move was viewed as a step toward liberating the networks from advertising control. Sylvester "Pat" Weaver had seized on the "magazine" approach to free the networks to put their own choices on the air, much as magazine editors select stories without regard to an advertiser's opinion. However, this "magazine" approach, ironically, may have harmed television's diversity. In the early days, a sponsor might present a program not to reach large numbers of people but for the prestige or the chance to reach a small, specific, devoted audience. Once the network took total control, however, and the game was to win the biggest possible audience at every moment of every day, the network literally could not afford to lose an audience for one hour; it might never get it back. So programs such as *Omnibus, Voice of Firestone,* and *The Bell Telephone Hour* went off the air or were cut back *despite* the willingness of sponsors to support them. The networks were engaged in a ceaseless battle for audience numbers and could not risk minority programming.)

RC cola provides an example of the way a product can "position" itself in a market through the people associated with the product. A contemporary RC cola campaign features attractive, young, natural-looking people in "natural," pastoral settings; those few who choose to stay in crowded, competitive cities have their own ways of staying loose.

The paper copier revolution in the American office was triggered by the Xerox copier. This 1962 commercial demonstrates that Xerox was such an easy machine, even a chimpanzee could operate it.

fancy music school in Boston; quitting an office job to buy a general store. (Some of the 1976 television commercials of Jimmy Carter and Gerald Ford employed the same rural-pastoral backdrops.) None of these campaigns represented a radical break with past advertising techniques; they were rooted in the half-century-old pattern of telling customers less about the product and more about their desires. The difference was that television, by definition, was able to flesh out fantasy projections more realistically than other advertising vehicles.

Many critics point to television advertising as a promoter of material acquisitiveness. That television advertising fuels a desire to buy, to consume, to be dissatisfied is a truism. But television's role in the growth of this desire was magnified because of the era in which the medium caught hold.

Network radio began in late 1926; three years later, America was hurtling into the Great Depression. And it went straight out of the Depression into World War II. In the Depression, there was not a huge amount of dis-

cretionary income. During World War II, there was not that much to buy. In other words, almost all of the first twenty years of network radio were times of economic constriction for most Americans. Television, by contrast, was introduced to an America that had just recovered from the war, ready to participate in the most explosive increase in the national standard of living that any society in history had experienced. From 1947 to 1960, ten million new households sprang up in America. From 1950 to 1960, the Gross National Product grew by $200 *billion*. By 1956, there were more white-collar workers than blue-collar workers in the country. An outpouring of products—from automobiles to suburban homes to frozen foods to electric appliances—flooded the marketplace.

Television advertising certainly fed this appetite. But television advertising did not create it. That appetite was created by a decade of depression and five years of war; it was inflamed by a thirst for material acquisition that the American economy was about to provide. Advertisers had found, to be sure, an ideal medium to reach a middle-class, increasingly suburban audience. But appetites grow independent of television, as was proved when cigarette advertising was forced off TV and radio in 1971—and sales continued to rise. The acquisitive fever that gripped America in the postwar years was reflected in television commercials, not created by them.

Television advertising has also been accused of being responsible for the packaging and selling of political candidates. Commercial spots for candidates quickly became a feature of elections after 1952, when Dwight D. Eisenhower's advertising agency, Batten, Barton, Durstine & Osborn, turned away from buying a block of time merely to broadcast a speech and, instead, presented sixty- and thirty-second spots, complete with cartoons, jingles, and Eisenhower's one-sentence answers to questions on inflation and national security. Political media consultants, who have become increasingly important in major election campaigns, experimented with every kind of advertisement, from testimonials given by ordinary citizens to carefully edited *cinéma vérité* presentations of a candidate talking and listening to ordinary folk. The sincere, into-the-camera appeal made famous by Richard Nixon's 1952 "Checkers" speech also found its way into the repertoire of political advertising. However the candidate is put forward on television, such advertising has become an integral part of the political process.

This kind of political advertising is overt. A more

178

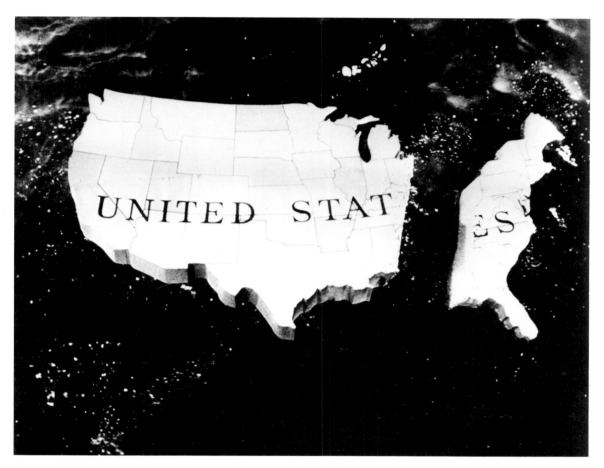

When a politician makes an embarrassing statement, a political television commercial can exploit that weakness. This 1964 Democratic ad graphically illustrates the remark of Republican presidential candidate Barry Goldwater that the Eastern seaboard of the United States ought to be "sawed off" the rest of the country.

A television taping crew headed by David Garth (partially hidden), one of the best-known political media consultants, tapes then-Congressman Hugh Carey for Carey's 1974 race to become governor of New York. Heavy use of television enabled Carey, who was known to about 6 percent of the New York electorate when he began, to win an upset landslide victory in the Democratic primary. He won another landslide victory in the general election.

Humor is a delicate tool in advertising; some experts claim the audience remembers the joke but not the product. In the mid-1960s, Alka-Seltzer *(top)* graphically illustrated the use of its product with film of different kinds of stomachs ("No matter what shape your stomach's in . . . "). In 1968, a creation of Stan Freberg employed the original TV Lone Ranger and Tonto (Clayton Moore and Jay Silverheels) to sell Jeno's pizza rolls.

central dilemma created by TV advertising was whether the *life-styles* they were "selling" had a political impact—that is, whether ads for products or for companies also contained messages about political or social matters. For example, if an oil company presented advertising that subtly ridiculed mass transit alternatives to the automobile or explained how important it was for oil companies to maintain "vertical integration"—ownership of all production and retail phases of operation—was that a simple ad? Or something more? If a food giant bought time in children's shows to sell sugared cereals, was that a simple pitch for customers? Or a message countering good nutrition?

The issue becomes important in light of a legal rule called the "fairness" doctrine. In brief, it requires broadcasters to provide equal access to the airwaves for competing views on important political and social matters. In 1972, the Federal Trade Commission recommended to the FCC that stations be required to provide "counter-advertising" when commercials contained controversial views on social, economic, and political matters. When this doctrine was applied to cigarette advertising, as a public health matter, cigarette advertising was eventually taken off the air. But what of a whole range of products that might contain debatable or controversial claims about the good life, or good eating habits, or consumer purchasing? This went beyond "truth in advertising"—the Federal Trade Commission was already making life hard for advertisers who put marbles in soup bowls to make the concoction richer looking (the marbles push the solid elements to the top) or who made unsupportable dietary claims for products.

This question was more complicated. If a product promised a more attractive complexion, could a public interest group demand time under the fairness doctrine to argue that the product in fact contained a carcinogen? If truckers bought time to proclaim the virtues of their service, could an antihighway or auto-safety group claim time to fight the truckers' implicit demands for new highway rules to permit bigger trucks on the nation's roads? When the war in Vietnam was at its height, a businessmen's antiwar group wanted to purchase time in order to argue against the war; all three networks refused the purchase offer on the grounds that the only acceptable political ads were on behalf of candidates for office.

Increasingly, advertising wraps its products around a life-style. So if advertising uses social and political symbols, does not the fairness doctrine provide a chance for a competing point of view? And if it does, what will happen to the economic structure of the television industry? Every interest group across the political spectrum understands that access to television is crucial to getting across a point of view. Interest groups such as Action for Children's Television had, by the mid-1970s, forced a dramatic cutback in advertising on children's programming, turning the former goldmine of Saturday morning cartoon shows into an area of marginal profitability. They had pressured networks into abandoning the practice of having children's show hosts like Captain Kangaroo hawk products and foods. These successes arose from an understanding that these commercials contained more than just a message to purchase a product. They contained messages about what was desirable and attractive to children. Would a parallel argument be extended into the world of commercials for adults? This is almost certain to become a central legal issue.

The argument is more complicated than the people-are-smarter-than-TV-critics-think response. For television advertising is now so expensive that commercials are designed far more carefully than ordinary messages or comments about a controversial issue. Production costs for a single thirty-second commercial can exceed $100,000. A single presentation of that commercial on a highly rated show will cost more than $50,000; on a show such as the Super Bowl, it will cost at least double that. Therefore, the combined efforts of market researchers, cameramen, sound men, graphic designers, writers, illustrators, actors, and directors are lavished on the creation of this thirty-second spot. Every second is crucial. Every foot of film is important. A camera crew may spend two weeks shooting a single commercial; they may wait for days for the perfect sunset to glint off a glass in just the right way; they may pour beer into a glass a hundred times or more to get precisely the right look. They will place the product in exactly the right environment, with exactly the right-looking people, to get the effect they want. For example, in the American Express Travelers Cheques campaign, Karl Malden is always wearing his hat, even indoors. Why? Because American Express wants the image of a tough, protective, law enforcement figure standing behind its checks. Malden has for many years portrayed just such a figure—who wears just such a hat—on *The Streets of San Francisco*. The hat reminds us of Malden's police image.

All of us have seen how a single commercial can

Hertz rents automobiles to time-conscious executives; using football star O. J. Simpson *(top)* to demonstrate speed and excellence is an effective match of personality and product. To prove its ability to please even the grumpiest customer despite its relatively small size, National Rent-a-Car uses insult artist Don Rickles *(center)*. For American Express, Karl Malden *(above)* is the embodiment of the law enforcement officer, the symbol of security an uncertain traveler wants in a traveler's check.

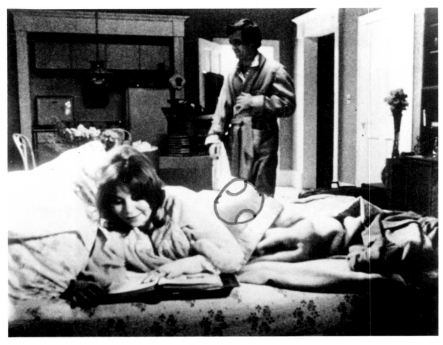

Two famous examples of commercials whose "characters" became famous overnight: the portly Southern sheriff *(top)* in the Dodge rebellion ad (played by Jim Higgins in this 1970 spot) and the newlyweds in Alka-Seltzer's "Groom's First Meal" commercial of the same year (Alice Playten played the bride; Terry Kiser played the groom).

implant an image across America almost instantly: the Dodge sheriff; the Alka-Seltzer newlywed couple; Barbara Feldon's Revlon tiger-skin girl; Farrah Fawcett-Majors's Noxzema shave cream sex kitten. Although these commercials reflect, rather than create, the longings of the American community, how is it possible to present an alternative view of America? At a trivial level, how does someone tell the American pet owner that pet food is a huge waste of money; that scraps from the family table can adequately feed a pet; that dogs do not have rampant lusts for cheese, onions, and garlic? At a deeper level, when a soap ad tells the consumer not to worry about greasy foods any more, who tells him that this may be true of his pots and pans but not of his cardiovascular system? Or that soap and water will adequately protect almost anyone from the painful social embarrassments depicted in deodorant ads?

Television is at one and the same time the American marketplace, the American polity, the American political and social forum. Access to that forum is determined almost exclusively by money—and the desire to spend that money on advertising a product. But television, by its very structure, cannot be segregated. When viewers watch a commercial in the middle of a news program or in the middle of an entertainment program, do they draw a line between information, entertainment, and a commercial pitch? Or does the sincere announcer in the commercial become the equivalent of the newscaster? Does the attractive sex object of a detective show blend in with the attractive sex object of the soap ad?

If television is part of the marketplace of ideas—as broadcasters argue when they seek to rid themselves of the fairness doctrine and other government regulations—then what happens if the marketplace is not free? What happens when the right to present a vision of this society is confined to those with a product to sell and the funds to sell it? Most Americans recoil at the prospect of a government agency making these decisions. But television advertising has demonstrated that it is so powerful, so bound up in images distinct from the simple selling of a product, and so effective in reaching the American populace that to leave it as the arbiter of American taste, preferences, and life-styles raises the most serious questions about the effect of television on democracy itself. By appropriating social values and life-styles in the service of salesmanship, advertising has become not just a tool to sell *things*, but a tool to sell visions of America itself.

Can an advertising campaign persuade people to go into a supermarket or butcher shop and ask for a brand of chicken? It can if the spokesman is Frank Perdue *(above)*, who owns the company. In the franchised fried chicken market, Colonel Sanders *(below)* represents Kentucky Fried Chicken, even though the Colonel sold the company to Heublein.

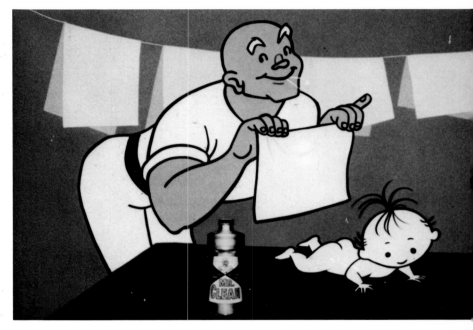

Three uses of fantasy to appeal to a buyer—in all cases here, to a predominantly female public. "Mr. Clean" *(top)*, the Ajax White Knight *(above)*, and the Jolly Green Giant *(left)* are all outsized male figures, communicating strength and masculinity—an appealing companion for a woman going through a daily routine of domestic chores without masculine help.

Jesse White portrays a Maytag appliance repairman who finds his work lonely because so few customers need to have their machines repaired. The campaign is a humorous way of making a claim that might be greeted skeptically at face value.

Charlie the Tuna (voice supplied by actor Herschel Bernardi) has for years been trying to join the Star-Kist company as food, only to be told that "Star-Kist doesn't want tuna with good taste, it wants tuna that tastes good."

He was a star for decades in plays and movies, but, Bert Lahr said near the end of his life, he was better known for his appearances in television commercials for Lay's Potato Chips than for anything else he ever did, including *The Wizard of Oz*, in which he played the Cowardly Lion.

Volkswagen's advertising campaigns were among the most successful in using humor as a selling tool. Here a devoted nephew *(below)* weeps on his way to his uncle's funeral, not knowing that his thriftiness in choosing a VW has earned him his uncle's $100 billion fortune. A stripped-down VW that got enormous mileage *(above)* was the company's way of poking fun at the exaggerated mileage claims of competitors.

DAYTIME

Passion
Once
Removed

Local stations often "counter program" network offerings of daytime dramas and game shows with midday talk shows. *Panorama* airs on an independent local station in Washington, D.C. Here, host Pat Mitchell (right) talks with actress Hermione Gingold and Georgia politician Julian Bond.

It is not entirely fair to describe daytime television as the exclusive preserve of soap operas and game shows—not entirely.

For local commercial independent stations—those not affiliated with one of the three commercial networks—daytime provides a chance to compete against network fare by offering their own public affairs and discussion shows, some of which (*Midday* in New York, *Panorama* in Washington, D.C., to name two) attempt serious discussion of public and personal concerns. In the morning hours immediately following network talk shows, some local station affiliates often endeavor to retain the *Today Show* or *Good Morning, America* audiences by presenting their own talk shows. The informal, easygoing talk shows of the Mike Douglas–Dinah Shore variety are frequently used as midday offerings. Both old movies and reruns of popular network shows such as *All in the Family* and *Sanford and Son* have also found daytime slots on the networks (reruns) and independent stations (movies).

As a rule, though, it is true that between 10 A.M. and 4 P.M. on a weekday, the twenty-five million regular viewers of daytime television choose between two forms: the daytime drama, popularly called the "soap opera," and the game show. Interestingly, they are linked to each other by ties much stronger than the fact that they are telecast during the daylight hours. They are the most enduring of broadcast forms, not only surviving but flourishing despite the fact that they are broadcast five days a week, and have been for more than forty years. They are throwbacks to earlier times, incorporating none of the technological breakthroughs that enabled television to leave the studio for the wide open spaces. Both game shows and daytime dramas are produced in virtually the same settings they used more than twenty-five years ago. Watching them, one is transported back to the early days of network televi-

sion. Only the use of videotape instead of live production, and the content of some of the soaps would give a viewer any clue that television was not in its infancy.

Most important, both the game show and the soap opera incorporate an appeal to their audiences' thirst for some kind of passion, even the vicarious variety, and to their need for a sense, however artificial, of dramatic peaks in the lives of "real" people. Whether this appeal is made through the frenzy of a game show or the never-ending chain of crises confronting the good folk of the soap operas, these daytime shows work only when they touch a viewer's concern. In intent, they are no different from the regular offering of prime-time shows. Only their budgets and their creators' perception that they must be paced to a different level of attention make them seem more ludicrous. Prime-time television is watched when the work is done and the children are either abed or themselves glued to the set. Daytime television, by contrast, must compete with the housework, telephone conversations, and other diversions of the housebound. No wonder the soap operas slow down real time, extending an hour's conversation over several days to permit the temporarily absent viewer to catch up. No wonder the game shows are ablaze with flashing lights, screaming participants, high-pitched music, and sound effects, all designed to capture the attention of an otherwise distracted audience. Moreover, these shows cannot employ the production values of prime-time television; the smaller audiences, and the lower advertising rates networks can thus charge, make economies imperative.

And so efficient are these economies that, despite the much smaller size of the daytime audiences, daytime television, since 1970, has been as profitable for networks as prime time—occasionally outperforming even prime time as the single most profitable time

period of all. With a network paying more than $150,000 for a single half-hour program on prime time and less than *half* of that for *five* half hours of soaps or game shows, the enormous profitability of daytime television becomes apparent. What may be less apparent to the observer who is not caught up in the web of daytime programming is why soap operas and game shows have such drawing power. Consider, then, the different ways that these two forms blend reality and fantasy to attract an audience.

In its original incarnation, the game show was really a panel show. On both radio and television, shows such as *Information Please, Twenty Questions, This Is Show Business* all used well-known, frequently witty and erudite highbrows or upper middlebrows (George S. Kaufman, Clifton Fadiman, Bergen Evans) to impart a blend of knowledge and amusement. This kind of panel show has disappeared; so have the game shows in which the "ordinary" players competed for trivial stakes. *What's My Line?,* the longest running of

The game show where the game is much less important than the quips of the celebrity panelists is an enduring television form. *What's My Line? (opposite page),* the progenitor of the form, ran for more than twenty years. Here, moderator John Daly appears with Dorothy Kilgallen, Louis Untermeyer, Arlene Francis, and Joey Adams. *I've Got a Secret (above)*, hosted by Garry Moore, was essentially the same show. The panelists pictured here are Bill Cullen, Jayne Meadows, Henry Morgan, and Betsy Palmer. *To Tell the Truth (below)* was a similar show, with a twist: three people presented themselves as "the *real* John Doe." Bud Collyer hosted the show. The panelists are (from left) Polly Bergen, John Cameron Swayze, Hildy Parks, and Hy Gardner.

Two modern versions of the game show where the game is relatively unimportant are the long-running *The Hollywood Squares (left)*, in which celebrities give rehearsed humorous answers to the questions, and *Celebrity Sweepstakes*. Note the visually "busy" sets; along with music, lights, and wildly cheering audiences, they are designed to compete with household work for the attention of the daytime viewer.

◄ *Password*, which debuted in 1961, was an innovative game show because it teamed an "ordinary" person with a well-known celebrity. Pictured here are host Allen Ludden and guest Peter Lawford playing the word-association game.

all such shows, awarded the successful player all of fifty dollars; the whole point was to watch elegant, sophisticated New Yorkers, folks like Bennett Cerf and Dorothy Kilgallen and Arlene Francis, being gay and amusing.

Today, a successful game show must offer at least two elements: an amiable, attractive, masculine host, and ordinary people with a chance to earn a reasonably impressive sum of money or goods. Some of the shows feature celebrities either playing a game with the ordinary person (*The $20,000 Pyramid, Password*) or playing off the ordinary people (*The Hollywood Squares, Celebrity Sweepstakes*). Often game shows need no celebrities at all. *The Price Is Right*, especially in its original form in the late 1950s with host Bill Cullen, so effectively whipped the contestants to a frenzy of lust and greed that a star would have been trampled in the rush to fondle the refrigerator. Shows

One of the earliest and most enduring celebrity game shows was Mike Stokey's *Pantomime Quiz (left)*, a charades game that was a perennial summer replacement show in television's early days. This 1952 contest shows (from left) Arleen Whelan, Barbara Rush, Richard Arlen, Mike Stokey, and Forrest Tucker. *Masquerade Party (below, left)* was a CBS nighttime game show in which panelists tried to guess the identity of a heavily costumed guest. Douglas Edwards was host of this 1953 panel.

One of the easiest satirical targets is the television game show that forces the audience-contestants into ludicrous situations in return for prizes. *Truth or Consequences*, inherited from radio, enjoyed tricking contestants into embarrassing their bosses and performing other stunts. The host, second from left, was Ralph Edwards.

Beat the Clock, hosted by Bud Collyer (this 1950 picture is from the show's earliest days), resorted to pie-in-the-face stunts; contestants had to carry whipped-cream pies on their heads for fifty seconds, among other things.

Chuck Barris, who created some of daytime television's most successful invasions of privacy (*The Dating Game, The Newlywed Game*), created and hosts *The Gong Show*, which takes the "Amateur Hour" format to an extreme of black humor by presenting acts deliberately chosen for their lack of talent or their grotesque qualities.

The naked avarice of contestants works as a game show premise. *The Price Is Right*, here shown in its modern version, *The New Price Is Right (below)*, with host Dennis James, has been successful because it lets the audience watch contestants go through a range of emotions as they lust after high-priced goods. *Let's Make a Deal (left)*, starring Monty Hall (center), took the premise a step further: Would you trade the prize you've won for what's behind the curtain? It could be a new car—or a worthless prize (a "zonk"). This type of suspense was first used in the old *Treasure Hunt* game show of the 1950s, but *Let's Make a Deal* honed the concept to a fine sadistic edge.

that can tap the frenzy of ordinary folk caught up in the chance for the big payoff can survive without the lure of celebrity. *Let's Make a Deal, Treasure Hunt,* and *The New Price Is Right* all fit this category. Surely the unquestioned apotheosis of such shows was *Supermarket Sweep,* which appeared in 1965 through the good offices of David Susskind. It gave contestants three minutes to clean as much off the shelves of a supermarket as possible. Husbands and sons wheeled the carts while the wives screamed encouragement from the checkout counter.

The amiable, attractive, masculine host is as essential a part of the fantasy as the payoff. He—as of this writing, there is no quiz or game show that has successfully installed a female host—is the romantic element in the fortune-and-romance formula common to all of these shows. For until the sex roles change far more drastically than is even now the case, the daytime audience will remain overwhelmingly female; therefore, the fantasy-hosts must be exclusively male.

That these shows flourish in daytime—and in the first half hour of prime time, through first-run syndication—despite the notorious quiz show scandals that exploded in 1958 and 1959 when they were dominating prime time testifies to the appeal inherent in putting ordinary people into crisis situations. (In a different form, this is the exact formula for a successful soap opera.) The original conception of men like producer Louis G. Cowan, who put as many as twenty quiz shows on the air in the late 1940s and early 1950s, was to make knowledge attractive by packaging it well. Such shows as *Quiz Kids,* a radio and television success, were designed to offset the anti-intellectual pressures that discouraged learning. But the formula that Cowan hit on in *The $64,000 Question,* which he brought to Revlon and CBS in 1955, and that was extended to *The Big Surprise, Twenty-One,* and *The $64,000 Challenge,* was very different. The size of the stakes, contrasted with the "typical" backgrounds of the contestants, set up a degree of tension that embroiled the entire country. It was also to prove the downfall of the quiz show as a prime-time format.

The premise of *The $64,000 Question*—the essential premise of so much of prime-time drama—was to focus in on personality, to find the quirk hiding within these "ordinary" real-life contestants by thrusting them into an atmosphere of tribunal-like solemnity, complete with isolation booth and uniformed security guards to "insure" honesty. A shoemaker who was an expert on grand opera; a grandmother whose field was baseball; a marine who was the first to win the big

Human suffering has always been an attraction of daytime television on the soap opera, but it was also exploited by two early television game shows. *Strike It Rich (top)* took desperate folk—those who needed a place to live, an operation, expensive medicine—and gave them money and prizes, some of them donated by publicity-conscious merchants or good-hearted viewers via the program's on-the-air "Heartline." Host Warren Hull (right) and hostess Jane Wilson here welcome a guest. On *Queen for a Day (above),* an NBC show hosted by Jack Bailey, suffering was fused with competition as four women battled for the highest share of audience sympathy in order to gain the crown and prizes.

The General Electric College Bowl, a throwback to the *Quiz Kids* idea of making knowledge exciting, pitted two teams of college students against each other in a contest of minds, not brawn. Allen Ludden was the host of the show.

In the late 1950s, quiz shows succeeded in prime time by providing huge cash prizes and battles between "personalities." This NBC publicity photo *(above)* of *Twenty-One* shows host and coproducer Jack Barry flanked by two contestants, Vivienne Nearing and Charles Van Doren, who had jousted for several weeks. But in October, 1959, Van Doren was caught up in what would become television's biggest scandal: the rigging of the shows. In this New York press conference *(top)*, Van Doren refused to make any substantive comment—but a few days later in Washington, D.C., he admitted he'd been given the answers to the questions.

prize—in the field of cooking; a woman psychologist who triumphed with boxing; a twelve-year-old boy who was an expert on the stock market: it was the players as much as the game that hypnotized America. And for prime-time sponsors, that was the problem. Contestants could not engage the audience simply by winning; they had to be personally attractive as well. And if they weren't? If they kept winning, but alienated the audience?

Charles Van Doren answered that question before a congressional committee in 1959, after confessing that he had been fed the answers to questions on *Twenty-One* throughout his "ordeal," although he had grimaced, sweated, and agonized his way through apparently impossibly difficult questions. He told the committee that the producer of the show had said that Herbert Stempel, the reigning champion, "was an 'unbeatable' contestant because he knew too much. He said that Stempel was unpopular, and was defeating opponents right and left. . . ." So Van Doren, a boyishly attractive intellectual, was given the answers to defeat the dumpy, arrogant Stempel. Similarly, the Revlon company was pressuring the producers of *The $64,000 Question* to force dull contestants off the air and to encourage more attractive ones. Ironically, Dr. Joyce Brothers, regarded by Revlon as too lifeless to appeal to an audience, not only won the top prize by virtue of a photographic memory but went on to become a successful media personality.

This situation had developed because the engineers of these shows looked upon them as entertainments whose pretensions of honesty were no more important than those of dramatic shows. James Arness wasn't *really* a sheriff in Dodge City; Robert Young wasn't *really* Jane Wyatt's husband; so why should Charles Van Doren *really* know the answers to all those questions? These producers, in other words, were applying the values of prime-time television to a form that could not honestly embody those values.

In the daytime arena, however, quiz and game shows could indeed survive. The contestants were screened to make sure they were as "ordinary" as possible. One show, which made a practice of using graduate and law students as contestants, told the players to list their last job, whatever it was, to preserve the illusion of "ordinariness." The daily scheduling of the shows, plus rules to keep a flow of contestants moving through, guaranteed that no cults of personality would develop—except around the host or the celebrities. (Here, too, spontaneity could not be trusted. On *The Hollywood Squares,* where funny

The soap opera—or daytime drama—was born in the early days of network radio. Many of the shows lasted not for years but for decades. *Ma Perkins (left)*, one of the first soap operas, began in 1933; it starred Virginia Payne as the folk-wise Ma Perkins, Murray Forbes as Willy Fitz, and Charles Egelston as Shuffle Shober. *The Romance of Helen Trent (center)*, also starting in 1933, ran for twenty-seven years by affirming that a woman over thirty-five could indeed find romance. Bill Green, Virginia Clark (as Helen Trent), Bill Farmer, and Louise Fitch (left to right) were members of the original cast. *Our Gal Sunday (right)*, beginning in 1937, was on for twenty-two years. Vivian Smolen played the orphan girl from a small Colorado mining town who married Lord Henry Brinthrope (played by Karl Swenson).

answers to questions are supposed to precede the real answers, the inevitably clever Paul Lynde and his cohorts are told what questions to expect. Since the contestants are kept in the dark, there is no real fraud.) There was no longer any pretense of erudition, no attempt to argue that these shows were an attractive method of engaging an audience in discourse or wit. That function, in revamped form, has been passed on to the talk shows of Carson, Griffin, Douglas, Shore, and their local progeny. What we are left with is a blend of reality and fantasy—real people are dropped into a fantasy/crisis environment (where nothing really bad can happen to them save for the failure to win big), surrounded by excitement and glamour, and given the chance at sudden riches. And it works.

The soap opera works in reverse; the people are fictions, but the crises they face—and face, and face, and face—are very real. Believability comes not from surrounding ordinary people with glamour, wealth, and prizes, but by subjecting imaginary people and places

to "real-life" problems, in melodramatic form. In direct contrast to prime-time dramatic series where a resolution is required at the end of each sixty-minute episode, the essence of the daytime drama is that there is no permanent resolution. There are always troubles, dilemmas, conflicts, crises.

The soap opera was not born in New York or Hollywood but in Chicago, during the early years of network radio. The success of *Amos 'n' Andy* in 1928 sparked a search for episodic radio shows, and in 1930, according to soap-opera historian Robert LaGuardia, Irna Phillips began writing *Painted Dreams* for a local radio station. The format caught on, and shows such as *Ma Perkins, The Romance of Helen Trent,* and *The Story of Mary Marlin*—the first of many by Frank and Anne Hummert—flooded the airwaves. The form was a natural for television, especially in the early days when bulky live cameras and cramped studios forced action indoors to concentrate on the conversational and the intimate. As early as 1942, a

For more than a quarter of a century, Mary Stuart has starred as Joanne Tate (*née* Barron) in *Search for Tomorrow*, which has been on CBS since 1951. In this photo from that first year *(below)*, Lynn Loring plays her daughter Patti. In a later story development *(right)*, Jo's sister Eunice (played here by Ann Williams) married her boss John Wyatt (played by Val Dufour) following her first husband's death after a series of disasters.

Another CBS stalwart, and the first serial to grow from fifteen minutes to a half hour, is *As the World Turns*. The Hughes family is at the center of this soap; in a 1959 picture *(above)*, Chris, Nancy, and Pa Hughes (as played by Don MacLaughlin, Helen Wagner, and Santos Ortega) appear. Rosemary Prinz played the Hugheses' daughter Penny, shown with Helen Wagner *(above, left)* in this 1956 picture. Chris and Nancy are still together *(left)* in this 1976 photo. The Oakdale-based story also focused on Dan and Susan Stewart *(right)*, played by John Reilly and Marie Masters.

An early NBC effort to counter CBS's primacy in soap operas, *Hawkins Falls*, lasted for four years. It experimented with scenes filmed outdoors in contrast to the studio-based soap operas that are still dominant.

For forty years, on radio and television, *The Guiding Light* has been a daily staple of daytime programming. In this 1952 photo, Theo Goetz plays Papa Bauer and actress Charita Bauer plays the ever-suffering Bert.

These long-running serials are no longer on the air. *A Brighter Day* ▶ *(top)*, which began on radio in 1948, went to television in 1954 and ran until 1962. In this scene from the show's last year, June Dayton played Patsy Dennis; Mike Barton was her son, Chris Hamilton; and Paul Langton played Patsy's uncle, Walter Dennis. *The Secret Storm (center)* ran for twenty years until its 1974 cancellation. In this 1970 photo, Linden Chiles and Marla Adams appear as Paul and Belle Britton. *Love Is a Many Splendored Thing (bottom)* ran from 1967 to 1973, with the emphasis on young loves and losses. This 1972 photo shows senatorial candidate Spencer Garrison (played by Ed Power, left) arriving at his campaign headquarters. Leon Russom, Albert Stratton, Gloria Hoye, and Barbara Stanger (left to right) play his friends and campaign workers.

Younger than only *Search for Tomorrow, Love of Life* premiered on television in 1951. Jonathan Moore and Diane Rousseau *(left)* play the obviously concerned Charles and Diana Lamont in this mid-1970s photo. This 1959 picture *(right)* shows director Larry Auerbach (left) with actors Ron Tomme and Audrey Peters, as Bruce and Van Sterling; all were still with the show in 1977.

Under the guidance of Agnes Nixon, the creative queen of ▶ daytime drama, *Another World* was the first soap to go to a full hour, in 1975. Here Victoria Wyndham, left, as Rachel Corey, is shown with Irene Dailey, as Aunt Liz.

soap called *Last Year's Nest* was telecast in Philadelphia, and in 1950, CBS began *First Hundred Years.* By 1952, such staples of daytime television as *Love of Life, Search for Tomorrow,* and *The Guiding Light* were on the air (the last has been on network radio or television continually for *forty years*).

The sheer longevity of these shows is remarkable. On prime-time television, fewer than half of all new shows last out their first year. A show that runs five years or more is considered an exceptional hit. Yet on daytime television are progams, broadcast five days a week, that have run continually for more than twenty years. Such principal actors as Mary Stuart, in *Search for Tomorrow,* have been on for more than a quarter of a century.

What has surprised—and in recent years impressed—the scoffers, who have traditionally laughed at the endless stream of diseases, amnesia attacks, disappearances, adulteries, heartbreaks, divorces, and miscarriages on the soaps—is the degree to which these dramas have incorporated a sense of realism about their characters and society into their forms.

For almost fifteen years, *The Doctors* has demonstrated the ▶ natural dramatic appeal of the life-and-death work of the medical profession. Here Elizabeth Hubbard (right) plays Dr. Althea Davis and Lydia Bruce plays Dr. Maggie Powers.

One of the first sexually open daytime dramas was *Days of Our Lives*, which premiered in 1965. In the show, Bill Hayes plays Doug Williams and Susan Seaforth plays Julie Olson, about to become Julie Williams. In 1974, Susan Seaforth became Susan Hayes when she married her soap "husband."

As early as 1963, actor George C. Scott recognized that "the sense of growth and continuity has never been developed in broadcast series at all—except, interestingly enough, in the old radio soap operas." This principle has been extended to the television soaps. As in the daily comic strips that inspired the original soaps, characters grew: they married, had children, matured, even died. When an actor left a show, he did not simply disappear; his character was accounted for, by death, divorce, a change of career, or another event that might happen to someone in real life.

These events have always had a profound impact on the audience, which has seen and heard the people and their problems day after day for years on end. Soap operas receive thousands of congratulatory cards and letters when a favorite character "marries"; thousands of telegrams and sympathy cards are received when a character "dies." Evil characters are so detested by loyal soap watchers that the actors playing them have been vilified and assaulted in public; a loyal, suffering "spouse" will be warned by followers of these programs that his or her mate is carrying on behind his or her back.

Moreover, as the rigid moral limits on broadcasting drama were loosened, daytime drama characters began to experience the kinds of problems that were ignored by prime-time television until well into the 1970s. As partisans, including writer Dan Wakefield, have noted, the soap operas were the first broadcast dramas to touch on such subjects as adultery, impotence, alcoholism, drug addiction, venereal disease, mastectomies, and other once taboo topics. On the more contemporary soaps, such as *All My Children* and *The Young and the Restless,* women's liberation, antiwar protests, and wide-scale sexual promiscuity were incorporated as part of the plot line almost as a matter of course.

Curiously, it may well have been the special nature of the daytime audience that permitted such exploration years before it became possible to deal with these topics at night. The creators of soaps, led by Agnes Nixon, onetime protégée of Irna Phillips, recognized that they were speaking to an almost exclusively isolated audience, mostly female. It is an audience left at home, outside the mainstream of working people. This audience is used to grappling with personal, emotional crises in the lives of friends and neighbors. The kind of "male armoring" that considers open discussion of personal problems "weak" is largely absent from this audience. Further, the demands of the

In the most candid of all daytime dramas, *The Young and the Restless*, Dorothy Green and Robert Colbert play husband-and-wife Jennifer and Stuart Brooks.

One of the most popular of current soap operas is Agnes Nixon's *All My Children*, now on for an hour five times a week. Ruth Warrick plays Phoebe Tyler, shown *(below, left)* with Maureen Mooney. In a rare scene of relative tranquility *(below)*, Susan Lucci (playing Erica Kane), Nicholas Benedict (as Phillip Brent), Paulette Breen (as Claudette Flax), Chris Hubbell (as Charles Tyler II), and Stephanie Braxton (as Tara Martin) gather together.

prime-time dramatic series—the need for strong, supremely competent heroes who can resolve problems every week—all but preclude the expression of vulnerability. Indeed, it was one of the marks of a superior nighttime show like *Gunsmoke* that on occasion the hero revealed a more personal side of himself—a sense of weariness, a longing for love or peace. But the prime-time audience that looks scornfully upon daytime drama as unrealistic accepts the weekly, repetitive nature of prime-time drama unquestioningly.

Perhaps because of the movement and action of the higher-budget nighttime shows it was possible to disguise the inherently artificial nature of the characters and their lives. Mannix always got his man; Kojak never fails; Starsky and Hutch always bust the drug ring. But the people of Pine Valley (the setting of *All My Children*) and Hawkins Falls—and yes, even of Fernwood in the half-parody *Mary Hartman, Mary Hartman*—do struggle and fail, and learn to live with loss and disappointment and tragedy. The key to the

One of the first attempts to move the continuing-story format of soaps into prime time was *Peyton Place*, which ran twice and then three times a week at night on ABC in the early 1960s. Barbara Parkins and Ryan O'Neal were two of the series regulars.

In two years, Norman Lear's half parody, half tribute to soap operas, *Mary Hartman, Mary Hartman,* became a national fad and was then reshaped by its producer. Set in mythical Fernwood, Ohio, the show took a surreal approach to the soaps, but, wisely, the comedy was supplemented by a real story line. Louise Lasser played the anxiety-ridden heroine.

phenomenal first-year success of *Mary Hartman, Mary Hartman* (or *MH2*) was not just laughter; the viewers were both amused by the show and engrossed in the lives of the people. Even the one totally outlandish soap opera, the vampire- and ghost-laden *Dark Shadows,* succeeded because the audience somehow sympathized with Jonathan Frid's characterization of the tormented vampire, Barnabas Collins.

The daytime audience accepts this personal, drawn-out form of drama, so much so that the only presentation of "high-quality" drama in the daytime, NBC's *Matinee Theatre*, could not survive more than four seasons in the mid-1950s. Until the 1970s, however, networks assumed that the form could not be transplanted to nighttime when men, teenagers, and children are all part of the prime-time audience. The one successful attempt to present prime-time soap opera was *Peyton Place,* which appeared twice and then three times weekly on ABC in the mid-1960s. But as the 1970s began, a number of different pressures on the networks combined to bring the premises and values of daytime television into prime time.

The nation had just passed through the sixties, the most tumultuous decade of the twentieth century, which had assaulted all of America's cultural assumptions. Changes in political rhetoric, sexual conduct, generational obeisance, and adherence to customs had shaken America; television, through its news programs, was the conduit of the shock waves. The networks were seen less as carriers of an explosive series of upheavals than as the proponents of those upheavals. A longing for the "traditional" values of home and family was in the air. The public simply did not want "relevancy" in its entertainment programming; the spate of "relevant" shows in the late sixties—about young lawyers, young doctors, young rebels—sank almost without a trace. Finally, the explosion of violence in cities, on campuses, in American political life made violence on television a matter of urgent concern, especially as presidential commissions on riots and violence pointed a cautionary finger at the television industry.

So when Fred Silverman, then programming head of CBS, saw a made-for-TV movie called *The Homecoming* about a close-knit family surviving the Depression on a mountain in Appalachia, he suggested the idea of a series to creator Earl Hamner, Jr., and producer Lee Rich, neither of whom had had any idea of turning the movie into a series.

With the active encouragement of CBS chief William Paley, the show, called *The Waltons,* went on the air in

Martin Jarvis (as Jon) and Susan Hampshire (as Fleur) appear in a scene from *The Forsyte Saga*, a British import first broadcast on PBS in the fall of 1970. The show helped create the "mini-series" boom which flourished in 1976 and beyond on network television. The costumes and the literary origin of *The Forsyte Saga* (it was adapted from John Galsworthy's novels) helped cloud the soap-opera qualities inherent in the series.

September, 1972, partly because the time period was dominated by the competition—*The Flip Wilson Show* and *Mod Squad. The Waltons,* however, turned into one of the most popular prime-time shows, in large measure because of qualities that once would have been called "soap opera." There were no gunfights or car chases; there were moments of leisurely, uneventful conversations between siblings or between the younger and older generations. Instead of relevancy, there were explicit old-fashioned family values: a strong father, devoted mother, active and venerated grandparents (no nursing home here!), a life spent fulfilling obligations rather than pursuing pleasure.

And when *The Forsyte Saga* and *Upstairs Downstairs* succeeded on public television, the idea of a prime-time series in which major characters suffered and died became thinkable. CBS, with *Beacon Hill*, ABC, with *Rich Man, Poor Man* and *Roots*, and NBC, with *Captains and the Kings,* began to present primetime offerings in which—over a shorter, more intense story line—echoed some of the taken-for-granted

Family, a nonviolent nighttime drama, succeeded in creating the type of audience involvement gained by daytime drama. (Shown, from left, are *Family* members Kristy McNichol, James Broderick as the father, Sada Thompson as the mother, Gary Frank, Michael Shakelford, and Meredith Baxter-Birney.) There is little melodrama here, and the constant disasters afflicting soap opera characters are mercifully absent.

aspects of soap opera. Even without a continuing, constantly tense series of dramatic confrontations, prime-time television is reflecting a "soap-opera" sense of continuity when it runs a show like *Family*. The oldest daughter, a divorced mother of a young child, has affairs, considers remarriage, wonders what is to become of her life. The son is a dropout from school, trying to learn a skill, uncertain of what he wants to be. The youngest daughter grows into sexual maturity, struggles with conflicts between friendship and romance. The middle-aged parents flirt with adultery, worry about their children, each other, and their mortality.

It goes too far to say that the daytime dramas of television are genuinely realistic. The necessities of the form require too many brushes with the kinds of crises that most families would suffer only a few times in a generation. What must be acknowledged is that the hidden strengths of this form—hidden, that is, from the prime-time audience—have proven to be enduring, and useful in the attempt to move television closer to what Paddy Chayefsky once called "the marvelous world of the ordinary." The daytime television audience, out of choice or the lack of an alternative, has stayed with the convention of continuing characters in familiar settings. What the world of daytime drama has given prime time is the possibility of exploring such characters not through the prism of escape or fantasy action, but through a focus closer to the way most of us really spend our lives. And that is no mean contribution from a form as ridiculed as the daytime drama.

NEWS AND SPORTS

Bigger than Life

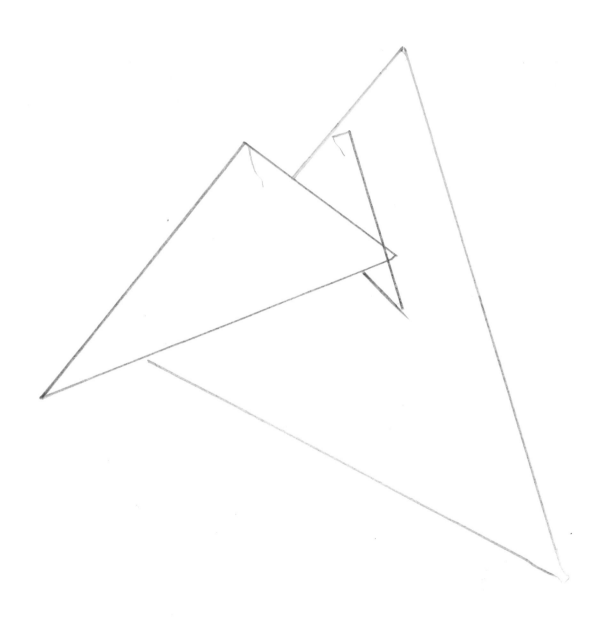

The relentless demand of television for the biggest possible audience has reshaped the medium. In the process it has reinforced some of radio's forms, dismantled the early dramatic possibilities of the medium, and honed in on the development of appealing characters, personalities, people to draw the audience to the show. In two areas of television coverage, however, the event itself was so much the center of attraction that the exploitation of the personal was, for many years, relatively rare. These two areas—news and sports—seemed to contain such inherent dramatic properties that they attracted audiences not for whom they featured, but primarily for *what* they featured: linking the Atlantic and Pacific oceans instantaneously; bringing the World Series to the half of the nation that had never seen a major league baseball game (until 1955, no major league franchise was located west of the Mississippi except for St. Louis); taking the viewers inside a Senate hearing in a Manhattan office building to watch the hands of a camera-shy witness toy with a pair of glasses; giving a closer view of the field of action than a seat on the fifty-yard line could give.

The presidential nominating conventions furnish a classic case of how television news moved from observer to active participant in the political process. The first conventions in which television was a full-fledged observer were those of 1952. Adlai Stevenson, as governor of Illinois, gave a witty, eloquent welcoming address at the Democratic convention *(opposite page, top)* that made him nationally known instantly. With the active assistance of President Truman, Stevenson became the Democratic presidential nominee.

By 1968, television coverage of the Democratic convention *(opposite page, bottom)*—and of the disturbances in the streets outside Chicago's convention hall—had become a national issue, with charges of distortions and unfair emphasis on police brutality. Richard Nixon's renomination at the 1972 Republican convention *(opposite page, center)* was almost totally staged for television; a prepared "script" even indicated when "spontaneous" demonstrations would erupt.

These contrasting views of the 1976 Republican convention illustrate television's supremacy. From the delegate's view *(top)*, little is clear; from the perch of the anchor booth *(above, left;* NBC's John Chancellor, left, and David Brinkley are shown here) the entire hall is visible, and information flowing in from all over the floor and the candidates' headquarters keeps the reporters up to date.

Politicians know that television takes the traditional "home and family" images and makes them exceptionally vivid. At the 1976 Democratic National Convention *(above)*, presidential nominee Jimmy Carter is surrounded by mother, daughter, sons, and wife.

Chet Huntley and David Brinkley were first teamed by NBC at the 1956 Democratic National Convention in Chicago. The combination of the somber Huntley and the witty Brinkley made them a highly successful anchor team when they replaced John Cameron Swayze on the network's nightly news show in the fall of 1956. Brinkley again became coanchor of the NBC evening news show in 1976.

overleaf:
Inevitably, those who reported the news on television became as recognizable, and as famous, as those whose activities they were reporting. Here, exchanging on-camera remarks during the 1968 Democratic convention (from right) are floor reporters Sander Vanocur, John Chancellor, Frank McGee, and Edwin Newman.

Five hundred feet away from the action at Yankee Stadium, a bleacher fan *(left)* gets closer to home plate via portable television. From the broadcast booth at the stadium, Mel Allen served as "the voice of the Yankees" from 1939 until 1964. Like many other sports announcers, Allen developed his own signatures: "Going, going *gone!*" to describe a home run and "How *about* that!" to describe an outstanding play.

placed John Cameron Swayze on the NBC news show in the fall of 1956.

But what had made them successful as a team? More or better news? Or something else? Dick Wald, currently president of NBC News, says that "after years of solemn reporters, here were two human beings who actually talked to each other." There was an appealing personality mix between the serious Huntley and the less inhibited Brinkley. By now, television had discovered that however much the news operation wanted to remain separate from the entertainment aspect of television, there were fundamental reasons why such a separation could not fully succeed. In part, it was because audiences used television as an entertainment medium. They could, in a newspaper, easily distinguish between the serious news and the comics, but television news was something that happened a few moments each day (networks were only broadcasting fifteen minutes until 1963), in between the shows. In part, it was that *anyone* who was on television every night, coming into the home, promoted feelings of both awe and intimacy. He or she was someone the viewer knew, trusted, liked, believed. Viewers were not likely to pick and choose among competing news programs on the basis of who explained the federal budget better. Once viewers recognized a threshold level of respectability and competence among the news shows—recognition that perennially eluded the younger, poorer, traditionless American Broadcasting Company—they would pick the people they most wanted in their homes. In the second half of the 1950s, that meant Huntley and Brinkley. And it also meant a growing realization among news executives that the bearer of the news was as important, if not more important, than the news itself.

In the field of sports as well, the late 1950s and early 1960s were significant, for sports executives discovered more about what the public wanted from a sports program—and why. In the 1950s, baseball was considered the national pastime. Football was then a sport best appreciated by collegians, and the pro game ran a poor second to baseball in its following. Basketball was a high school sport of fanatical followers, but pro ball had never built a league with staying power. And

◄ Professional basketball, long a stepchild of major league sports, was one of many sports that received multi-million-dollar infusions from network television. In this Knicks-Celtics game of the early 1970s, Dave DeBusschere shoots against Steve Kuberski, while Jerry Lucas looks on.

The packaging of sports and the networks' capacity to feed a seemingly insatiable appetite for more sports coverage led to the expansion of pregame and half-time shows. CBS developed *NFL Today* to provide pregame reports and features. Here, then-CBS Sports vice-president Robert Wussler chats with Phyllis George, the first successful woman sports commentator.

An early demonstration of the up-close ability of television was provided in this 1947 football game between two New York professional football teams, the Brooklyn Dodgers and New York Yankees. Yankee coach Ray Flaherty watched the game on television from the sidelines, looking for missed assignments and hidden angles.

An early attempt to educate the sports viewer was in this 1950 telecast. A white arrow or "electronic pointer" was used to show who was carrying the ball. In later years, instant-replay devices provided half a dozen views of the same play, in slow motion.

hockey, in the late 1950s, was a league with six teams in only four American cities, whose following was loyal but small. But baseball was not a sport well suited to the world of television. Its field of action was wide, diffuse; its most exciting plays, such as the extra base hit with men on base, could only be covered by fragmenting the action or by pulling the camera back so far that the players appeared antlike. In addition, there were 154 games a year, and many baseball teams permitted coverage of every home game as well as out-of-town games. In New York, which had three baseball teams until 1958, more than 400 baseball games were broadcast to the same community each year—and that was overexposure with a vengeance. One of the first things

Dodgers owner Walter O'Malley did when he moved the team from Brooklyn to Los Angeles was to black out home games; whether as a consequence or not, the Dodgers have been among the most successful baseball franchises almost every year since.

Football, by contrast, was a weekend sport exclusively. It was played in the autumn and winter, when the weather was more likely to keep people indoors. Both the college and professional seasons included a dozen games or less, so every game was crucial. And, in a burst of shrewdness, the National Football League had negotiated an agreement with CBS that flatly prohibited the telecasting of any home games. The road games therefore stimulated the fan's interest, which could be

226

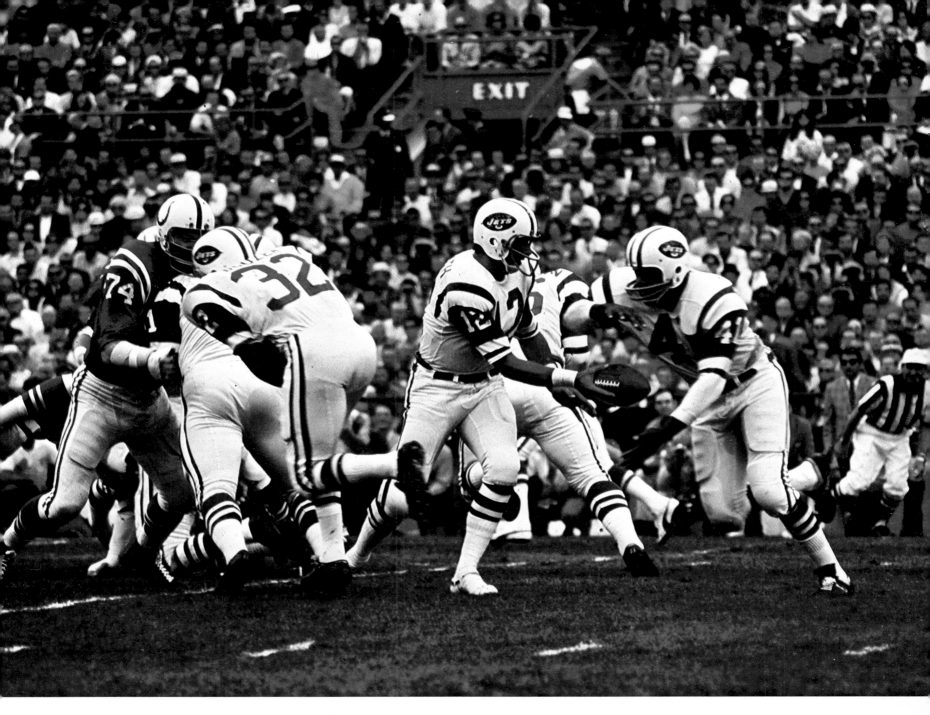

In 1969, the American Football League—which had been kept alive by a network television contract—proved itself equal to the older National Football League when the New York Jets upset the Baltimore Colts in the Super Bowl. Joe Namath, the swinging single Jet quarterback, became a six-figure spokesman for products long after his arm—and his team—stopped producing.

satisfied only by attending the home games in person. Further, in 1958, the New York media, deserted by the baseball Brooklyn Dodgers and New York Giants, who had both pulled up stakes for California, found in the New York Giants of the National Football League a new source of affection. The Giants returned the compliment by fighting the Baltimore Colts for the NFL championship in a sudden-death overtime game which many sports writers called "the greatest football game ever played." This hoopla fed the appetite of sports fans for professional football—a sport whose violent contact could be reached by the Zoomar lens, whose deceptive fakes, hand-offs, and quick cuts by running backs and pass catchers could be brought to the home

viewer in a manner inaccessible to the fan at the football stadium. From 1958 to 1969, the sport of professional football exploded. A newcomer, the American Football League, survived a dearth of spectators in the early sixties because of a $42 million, five-year contract it signed with NBC on the heels of the New York Jets' acquisition of Joe Namath. In the mid-1960s, CBS paid the National Football League $14 million a year for the rights to its games; in 1970, ABC bought the rights to *Monday Night Football* for almost $9 million a year.

College football, an exclusive province of ABC (save for the postseason bowl games), received a novel treatment under the direction of Roone Arledge, who was later to become president of ABC Sports. Rather

The 1976 Sugar Bowl—matching up Pittsburgh and Georgia—was one of many sports shifted into prime-time schedules over the years to maximize television audiences. The Sugar Bowl is now played in the New Orleans Superdome, where the vagaries of weather are overcome, so that—among other things—the television picture remains clear.

"The most trusted man in America," according to political polls, is Walter Cronkite, anchorman of *The CBS Evening News* since 1962.

than emphasizing the complexity of the game, Arledge began to focus on the *pageantry:* the faces of the cheerleaders, the intensity of the crowd. Hand-held cameras recorded close-up reactions of players on the benches, of coaches and officials, of members of the band as their team went down to defeat. Under Arledge's guidance, the coverage of college football beginning in 1960 underwent a fundamental change which was to alter the premise of television coverage of all sports. Instead of bringing the home viewer to the game, television was taking the viewer into a game, as an event with intense emotional involvement—which no spectator at a game could ever grasp. It was to become a much more intimate glimpse of sports than the "real" event could provide. It was beyond reality.

By the early 1960s, the basic form of what is now known as the nightly network news had taken shape. NBC was featuring Huntley and Brinkley, reporting from New York and Washington, D.C., respectively. In 1962, Walter Cronkite replaced Douglas Edwards as anchorman on the *CBS Evening News*. In 1963, Elmer Lower, hired away from NBC by ABC, began to make of that spit-and-baling-wire news operation a professional operation. That same year, both CBS and NBC news went to a half hour, with the tacit understanding that in most major markets the network news would be carried at the same time. (ABC did not expand its news to a half hour until 1967.) If either network had competed against news with an entertainment program, it would have wiped the news show off the ratings chart.

None of the networks could have put its news programs on the air, other than on the five stations around the country each of them owned and operated, through its own efforts. But, as Edward Epstein has documented in *News from Nowhere*, the Federal Communications

In 1963, Americans were mesmerized by television coverage after the assassination of President John Kennedy. The solemnity of the funeral *(top)* and the shocking murder of accused assassin Lee Harvey Oswald by Jack Ruby *(center)* were conveyed with a sense of immediacy and drama. Television also captured the shooting of Alabama Governor George Wallace *(bottom)* in the midst of his 1972 presidential campaign. Wallace's wife, Cornelia, comforts her wounded husband.

Commission in effect compels local network affiliates to carry network news by making national news coverage an important item in judging whether station licensees serve the public interest. And local stations simply find it cheaper to carry network news and documentary shows than to attempt to finance their own operations. Epstein quotes one NBC executive as acknowledging, "Without the FCC, we couldn't line up enough affiliates to make a news program or documentary worthwhile."

By the same token, the exploding profits in network television in the 1960s made the money-losing prime-time documentaries a less and less attractive commodity. Ed Murrow's *See It Now* had been eased out of the CBS prime-time schedule and consigned to the weekend "ghetto," to be replaced by the sometimes excellent, sometimes soft *CBS Reports*. (Murrow himself left the company with a good deal of bitterness in 1961 to become director of President John F. Kennedy's United States Information Agency.) This illustrates the double standard of the networks, which criticize their "money-hungry" affiliates while presenting a generally unbroken history of squeezing public affairs out of every conceivably profitable time slot.

However, changing conditions made the nightly news shows more financially attractive by the early sixties. The working population of America was coming home more and more by auto, less and less by mass transit, where the evening paper was a welcome companion. With a choice of three network news shows that were broadcast about the time working Americans got home, the demand for afternoon and evening papers was shrinking. No news in an evening paper could hope to compete in timeliness with network television news; and the launching of Telstar I in 1962, followed by other communications satellites, had made it possible to transmit news from anywhere in the world directly to a network broadcast center when events warranted. If anyone had any doubt about the power of television to communicate major events to the entire nation, it was dispelled forever during the four days from November 22 to November 25, 1963. Millions of Americans saw these scenes—the first bulletin that President Kennedy had been shot in Dallas, Walter Cronkite broadcasting directly from a CBS newsroom, the pomp of the funeral and the tributes, and, shockingly, the suspected assassin of John Kennedy, Lee Harvey Oswald, murdered on live television by Jack Ruby in the basement of the Dallas jail—as the country held vigil by its television sets.

Yet this very power was beginning to raise some bothersome questions. Take the simplest considera-

Almost unimaginable to an earlier generation, live television coverage from the moon was seen by 750 million people all over the world in the summer of 1969; it was the most witnessed event in world history.

Man wasn't there, but TV was, telecasting back to Earth the first photos from the planet Mars in 1976.

The first American to orbit the Earth, John Glenn, became an instant celebrity after his 1962 Project Mercury flight. Twelve years later, he became a United States senator.

Senator Sam Ervin and chief counsel Sam Dash are shown at the 1973 Watergate hearings. To preserve their daytime profits, networks rotated coverage of the hearings, except when moments of high drama, such as the testimony of former presidential counsel John Dean, were expected. Public television provided daily coverage throughout. The hearings made a national catchphrase of Senator Howard Baker's question, "What did the president know, and when did he know it?"

The line between news and entertainment is never fully clear on television. Tom Snyder, a news anchorman, appears on NBC's late-late-night show, *Tomorrow*. As an interviewer—here with Orson Welles—he fuses hard questions with a hyperbolic emphasis on sincerity.

Sometimes contentious, sometimes tendentious, David Susskind has been moderating a discussion show (*Open End*, later renamed *The David Susskind Show*) for almost twenty years. In this 1960 program, Susskind talks with members of the Soviet delegation to the United Nations.

The longest-running public affairs show on television is NBC's *Meet the Press*. Since 1947 public figures such as Ronald Reagan, shown here, have used this show as a forum to present their views.

tion—time. A thirty-minute newscast less commercials leaves twenty-two minutes to tell the American people of the important events that happened during the day. No one at the networks pretends that television news can be anything more than a headline service; in a famous experiment, CBS News executive Richard Salant printed the text of a typical nightly news show and it filled less than a full page of a metropolitan newspaper. Of course, this experiment proved little; after all, except for major metropolitan dailies, the typical newspaper does not have much after page one that is any more consequential than television entertainment. The more interesting question about time has to do with the na-

ture of a television news program. As with its entertainment offerings, a network must seek to draw the largest possible audience with its news program. And, as *Time*'s Thomas Griffiths has noted, "a crucial difficulty is that, unlike print, where the eye can skip around, you cannot jump to the broadcaster's next item, so each item must interest everyone a little and dare not go on long." To watch a television news program, then, is to be given a taste of information about a range of subjects in an order and package utterly controlled by the news show. Unlike a reader with a newspaper, a viewer is not in control of what he sees. He is instead at the mercy of a news show that cannot in any sense touch

The extensive network news coverage of the civil-rights movement—including this 1957 struggle to integrate Little Rock, Arkansas, schools—convinced some Southerners that television networks were biased in their news coverage.

on regional, cultural, or neighborhood distinctions, but, rather, has to present the most general kinds of stories.

It is impossible to say whether significant numbers of Americans would have grown to resent the power of television news had American society continued to be a politically placid arena. But with the explosive 1960s, Americans began to confront some hard issues. The civil-rights movement—sit-ins, freedom rides, voter registration marches—was covered by a national news-gathering operation overwhelmingly sympathetic to black demands. But these reports were carried to some regions with a sizable portion of the populace who were militantly against these demands. These viewers saw in network television not simply a recording of these events, but an advocacy of change. And such criticism was not confined to the South; as black demands grew, especially as they spread to the North, large numbers of citizens saw themselves in opposition to the protest movements being shown every night on the news. By 1964, their reaction could be seen in three Democratic presidential primaries *outside* the Deep South, as Alabama Governor George Wallace, then a strong segregationist, won 35 to 45 percent of the vote, making one of his major targets the national television networks.

This sense of resentment against the most visible and powerful of news organizations found fertile soil among other constituencies. The certainty among many that the entire national press corps was opposed to Barry Goldwater's candidacy for president in 1964—a certainty with a foundation in fact—produced in them a deep-seated resentment against the national press. And when the war in Vietnam began to escalate in 1965, it was the television networks, covering the war with few official restrictions, that brought to American homes pictures of the face of war that had never been shown before: not friendly troops welcomed by the populace, but troops setting fire to villages with cigarette lighters; troops cutting off the ears of dead combat foes; allies spending American tax money for personal gain. There was no way to turn the page, no way to ignore the news that was posing such a challenge to traditional assumptions about American participation in foreign conflicts. There was no way to ignore what network television was showing America—about the cities, the campuses, the war—but that did not mean it had to be believed. This credibility gap—not between president and people, but between people and their primary source of information—created the

The issue of unfair TV coverage exploded during the war in Vietnam, when TV brought into American homes the ugly side of war. Two of the most famous incidents televised were the burning of a Vietnam village by American troops (*top, left*; shown in an August, 1965, field report by CBS newsman Morley Safer) and the summary execution of a suspected Vietcong agent by South Vietnam's National Police Chief Nguyen Ngoc Loan (*left*) during the 1968 Tet offensive. Television was specifically accused of publicizing the growing demands of antiwar protesters (*above*) in the late 1960s.

opportunity for a national administration to make the network news a prime political target.

Richard Nixon's relationship with the press had never been warm; after his 1962 loss in the California gubernatorial election, he held his famous "last press conference" in which he pledged that the press wouldn't have Nixon to kick around anymore. (He also paid tribute to television news for keeping the written press honest.) When he and his aides took over the White House and a war in Vietnam they had not begun, they quickly made that war theirs, and saw in the broadcast press—"the media," they called it, instead of using the all-American word "press"—a committed opponent of the Nixon administration's policy. So White House speechwriter Pat Buchanan crafted a speech for Vice-President Spiro Agnew. Delivering it in Des Moines, Iowa, in November, 1969, Agnew attacked "a small group of men, numbering perhaps no more than a dozen anchormen, commentators, and executive producers, [who] settle upon the twenty minutes or so of film and commentary that's to reach the public" as "a tiny, enclosed fraternity of privileged men elected by no one and enjoying a monopoly sanctioned and licensed by government."

Several points need to be made. First, the Agnew attack—indeed, the overall White House offensive against the television network news departments—was explicitly political, based on the networks' practice of providing (in Agnew's words) "instant analysis and querulous criticism" instead of permitting Nixon to speak to the public without challenge. This was no principled assault upon concentration of media ownership, only upon those elements of concentrated power that provided opposing voices a chance to match the president's words. Second, the merits of the charge itself contained a substantial level of accuracy. In covering the 1968 Democratic convention, the networks *had* distorted reality by their timing in broadcasting the tapes of the police-youth confrontation in the streets of Chicago. There *were* only three national avenues by which to reach the public. And there was no real diversity in news presentation, no way to challenge Walter Cronkite's catchphrase that so irritated disaffected viewers and say to him, "No, that *isn't* the way it is, at least, not all of it."

And overarching all of these disputes was the undeniable fact that television news had become the focal point of the political process. This was symbolized by

In an effort to smother the press with access and affection, President Johnson invited the wives and children of reporters to attend an outdoor press conference in May, 1964 *(above)*. It did not succeed in bridging the "credibility gap" that helped erode Johnson's political popularity. After the Watergate revelations, President Nixon's press conferences *(left)* turned into emotional wrestling matches with the press.

In his November, 1969, attack on the broadcast media—carried live by all three ▶ television networks—Vice-President Spiro Agnew signaled the start of the most intense confrontation between a national administration and the press. The speech was followed up by repeated attempts to bring network broadcasting more in line with the policies, especially the foreign policies, of the Nixon administration.

In 1960, John Kennedy met Richard Nixon *(top)* in the first televised debate between presidential candidates. The more relaxed, telegenic Kennedy won the image battle, whatever the substantive point scoring. Sixteen years later, Jimmy Carter and Gerald Ford *(bottom)* met in a series of debates. They were sponsored by the League of Women Voters in order to avoid the equal-time laws preventing network sponsorship of debates. Here, television dominated the words and body language of both contenders.

The 1960 campaign of John Kennedy was built on an understanding of television. Here, in 1959, Kennedy appears on a Pittsburgh public affairs show hosted by Paul Long with high school and college students—one of hundreds of local TV appearances the underdog senator made. Kennedy demonstrated television's power to bypass the traditional party structure and reach the voters directly in their homes.

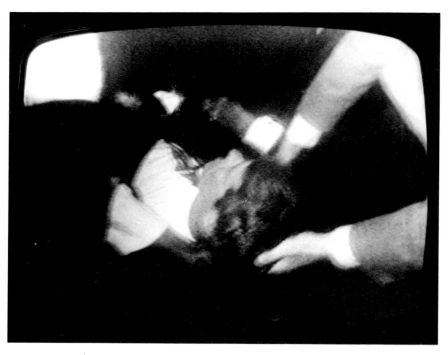

Television networks always had a camera crew near Senator Robert Kennedy in his 1968 presidential campaign; they anticipated an assassination attempt. When it came in June, 1968, in California, CBS's Jim Wilson was there to photograph the consequences.

the presidential debates between Vice-President Richard Nixon and Senator John Kennedy in 1960. The same Richard Nixon who had helped trigger a political revolution in 1952 by sitting down and speaking directly to the American people—face to face—in his famous "Checkers" speech had forgotten this lesson in 1960. In that first debate, Vice-President Nixon had looked at John Kennedy, at the moderator, at the studio audience—everywhere except the one place that counted: directly into the camera. The success of John Kennedy, in using television to overcome his youth and in bringing the force of his personality directly into the American home, was a new political phenomenon. Politicians at every major level began to realize that access to television could replace the traditional methods of gaining political power. Either through free television time or through heavy political advertising or a combination of the two, a politician could overcome the disadvantages of obscurity or rejection by the party establishment. Moreover, the continuing revolution in technology enabled television to cover politicians not just in halls with lighting and electrical outlets, but in factories, in private homes, anywhere a politician might choose to go in order to obtain an effective visual backdrop. In 1972, Democratic nominee George McGovern structured his entire presidential campaign to appear in three different media markets in the same day. And candidates were concerned less with the traditional forms of campaigning and more with the way they would appear on the evening news. The device that had begun by pointing at the traditional political processes had reshaped the nature of what it had intended originally to observe.

An analogous revolution in sports was also taking place through the 1960s and early 1970s. Sports had become a big-time, multi-billion-dollar industry, and television began to exert its inexorable influence to build the biggest possible audiences. The most obvious indication is the shift toward nighttime sports, since there are millions more people who watch television at night than during the day. So by the mid-1970s, traditional daylight events—the World Series games in midweek, the All-Star games, at least one professional football game each week—were shifted into prime time to gain bigger audiences and increased advertising revenues. Of course, by the time the World Series was played, what with four major league baseball divisions, a longer season, and playoffs, it was mid-October when nights get cool. But television was no longer an interested observer; it was an equal, perhaps senior partner with the game itself, spending millions of dollars for the rights to the World Series alone. Sore muscles and an occasional missed grounder because of the cold could hardly offset the power of the dollar.

A more fundamental change in the nature of sports was triggered by ABC's Roone Arledge in 1961, when ABC began broadcasting *Wide World of Sports*. At the time, the network had the rights to no major sports events save college football. It proceeded to create its own sports magazine, a two-hour show which broke with several existing conventions at the same time. Broadcast sports had always stressed its capacity to bring the viewer to an event as it was taking place; *Wide World of Sports* cut between live, taped, and filmed sports events, some of which had taken place days before in places around the world. Broadcasting had confined itself to traditional, major sports; *Wide World* covered everything from barrel jumping to stock car races to funny car auto-wreck championships—and drew large audiences as a result. The weekend sports audience, Arledge discovered, was interested in action, movement, spectacle. That it might be a sport viewers had never played, witnessed, or cared about before seemed not to matter. It was good television, and that was what counted.

The technological revolution had already shown audiences traditional games in totally untraditional ways. The isolated camera, the slow-motion instant replays, the pretaped interviews that were run as an athlete participated in an event had shattered the way the American viewer looked at sports. He was being bombarded with more visual data than a spectator at the game could see—resulting in the installation of huge television screens in some new sports arenas, affording the paying customer almost as good a view as the home viewer had. Further, the camera had brought the viewer far closer to an athlete than the paying customer, scrambling for an autograph after the game, could hope to reach. Before television, a sports event could only be witnessed as a spectacle—an event with competitors, *not* personalities. Television changed that, showing home viewers the faces behind the football helmets and close-ups of other athletes. Their private lives, contract battles, social and political views became as much grist for the gossip mills as had the lives of Hollywood stars a generation earlier.

In fact, so effective was television at turning athletes into celebrities that networks found they could create their own sports packages, which could outdraw traditional sporting events. In the early 1970s, CBS had pro-

Sports goes showbiz—in 1973, ABC telecast this "Tennis Battle of the Sexes" between Bobby Riggs and Billie Jean King. Ms. King won in three straight sets. More significant was the ability of television to package its own sports event, irrespective of the intrinsic athletic competition.

Sports and celebrities —they go together. Here a scene from the Bob Hope Desert Classic, with the comedian himself and golfer Doug Sanders.

Mark Spitz (right) won seven gold medals as a United States swimmer in the Olympics of 1972—he's shown here after helping to capture the 4 x 100 meter medley swim—but his attempt to parlay that triumph into a television career, as an actor and commercial spokesman, fizzled. Jean-Claude Killy (above), who was a star of the 1968 Winter Olympics at Grenoble, was far more successful as a television personality.

The mixture of sports and celebrities has become a more frequent offering of networks. Here Farrah Fawcett-Majors meets Bill Cosby in a 1977 CBS package called "Challenge of the Sexes," which includes battles between celebrities as well as athletes.

fessional basketball and NBC had major league hockey on Sundays. ABC created an artificial "Superstars" competition, with athletes competing in a kind of decathlon marathon, and drew the lion's share of the Sunday sports audience. By the mid-1970s, networks had begun to replace the existing sports structure with "Team Superstars," "Challenge of the Sexes," and a raft of other such events based on the premise that a viewer would watch a well-known personality in some form of competition regardless of the level of the game. Whether it was Jimmy Connors battling Ilie Nastase or Farrah Fawcett-Majors battling Bill Cosby on the tennis courts, the audience wanted to see *stars*, and the dividing line between athletes and entertainers was all but eradicated. The trend toward booking celebrities reached some kind of high—or low—in 1977 when CBS broadcast "Evel Knievel's Death Defiers," featuring Evel Knievel attempting one of his motorcycle jumps. The show drew high ratings, even though Knievel had injured himself in a practice run. The network apparently

Television was criticized for glorifying Evel Knievel, the daredevil motorcycle rider. Knievel is seen here leaping fourteen buses on an ABC appearance.

A helicopter helps put an ABC camera into position for the 1976 Winter Olympics at Innsbruck, Austria. ABC won critical praise for the unprecedented angles and beauty of its TV coverage of the Olympics.

The opening ceremony of the 1976 Winter Olympics at Innsbruck. ABC emphasized the color, pageantry, and the personalities of the athletes more than ever before.

Television propelled an obscure Rumanian gymnast into worldwide prominence literally overnight. The perfection and personality of fourteen-year-old Nadia Comaneci captivated viewers of the 1976 Summer Olympics at Montreal.

Muhammad Ali, then-unseated heavyweight champion thanks to a dispute with the government over draft resistance, plays with Howard Cosell's toupee in a 1972 appearance. Cosell, who defended Ali, gained a national reputation as a "controversial" sports announcer, who, in his own words, liked to "tell it like it is."

felt this presentation had crossed the line, and canceled its option on a second show.

Televised sports began by showing viewers an event they would otherwise have missed; it began by observing a real-life contest between highly skilled competitors as it was occurring. Its technological genius enabled it to cover these events with a new eye—to place cameras at the Olympics in such a way that the brilliance of a skier or a gymnast or a runner could be brought closer to a viewer than ever before in history. It was possible to see Nadia Comaneci balancing in midair, to see her footwork, her facial expression, her body control all at once. Sports and television, in this sense, seemed made for each other.

But the appetite of the viewers for the personal glimpse had extended beyond reality. They demanded more than skill; they demanded charm, wit, eloquence, and controversy as well. When ABC televised the 1976 Olympics, the network showed not just what a runner could do, but where that runner came from, how he or she lived; it brought the viewers, in the words of the network, "up close and personal." The question remains whether this emphasis on who an athlete is rather than what he can do on the field is covering sports—or smothering it.

It was perhaps inevitable that sooner or later television would personalize not only those it covered but also the people doing the coverage. As television reporters discovered with the growth of television news, a face frequently on camera becomes as well known as that of any politician or "celebrity." Network regulars—Walter Cronkite, David Brinkley, Chet Huntley, John Chancellor, Harry Reasoner—found it increasingly difficult to cover a campaigning politician, since the crowds gathered not around the politician but around the reporters. What was less inevitable was the deliberate attempt to attract viewers, specifically on the level of local television news, by emphasizing the personal attributes of reporters.

This trend had its unintended roots in an innovative news show on KQED, a northern California public television station. In the late 1960s, attempting to break with the rigid formula of local news, the station introduced *Newsroom*, a one-hour local show in which reporters sat around a horseshoe-shaped table and talked with each other about the stories they were covering. As the reporters combined their factual presentations with a more conversational approach to news, this enabled other reporters to bring up and clarify points that might be confusing to the viewer as well.

The *appearance* of this process, without much of the substance, materialized on local newscasts at the end of the 1960s, triggered principally by the *Eyewitness News* format of the ABC-owned and -operated stations. Here the news personnel were made the focus of the presentation. Instead of cutting from a news report to a commercial and then to the sportscaster, the anchorman exchanged "cross talk" with the weatherman ("Gave us a beautiful day yesterday, Pete, can you do it again today?") or sports reporter ("Hey, Biff, what's the matter with our Rams?"). On a lighter story, a reporter became *part* of it; for example, a reporter would end a story on a costume exhibition by donning a costume. A touch football game report would end with the reporter signing off, picking up the football, and throwing a pass. An anchorman also "quizzed" a reporter after a story, less to make substantive additions than to create the image of involvement ("Dan, do they know *why* the principal went berserk?" "Not yet, Bob").

These newscasts were structured around the premise that the television audience, whether for news or entertainment, was looking for the same values: action, pace, involvement, people to believe and care about. The promotional ads for New York's *Eyewitness News* showed the reporters and anchormen in each other's

In the early days of television, a woman's place on the news was confined to light features and an appearance as a "weathergirl." Shown is Jeanne Parr, a weathergirl on the *CBS Sunday News* in the early 1960s.

The local news team as "happy family" on one of the ABC-owned and -operated stations using an "Eyewitness News" formula, Los Angeles station KABC-TV. Shown from left are Jerry Dunphy, anchor, Eddie Alexander, Dr. George Fishbeck, weatherman and raconteur, and anchor Christine Lund.

communities—attending a wedding or an ethnic festival, teasing each other, laughing with each other. The shows open with the news team walking—or jogging—onto the set, to create a sense of motion. Some local news shows, as if they were a situation comedy instead of a news program, began to deliberately develop on-camera character traits of reporters and news readers: a "feud" between anchorman and sportscaster, a flirtation between anchorman and entertainment critic.

The search for the winning news format was understandable; by the mid-1970s, local news was an enormously profitable venture, accounting for a third to a half of a local station's profits. Local newscasts were routinely one-hour long in the bigger cities, with ninety minutes and even two hours a growing pattern in the biggest media markets. To the local news directors, under intense pressure to produce the highest ratings for the highest dollar—knowing that a single rating point could make a million-dollar difference in advertising revenues—it was crucial to develop winning news personalities and formats. Increasingly, they turned to news consultants (Frank Magid and McHugh and

Hoffman, Inc. being the two most famous companies), who would study an operation and recommend specific changes, usually shorter stories, a greater number of stories, more use of action film, more warmth and friendliness on the set. Many local stations began to hire reporters with no journalistic experience, looking only for the charismatic face and voice that would pull the audience to their stations at six and eleven o'clock. This trend led CBS's Charles Kuralt to observe that his overriding impression of local newscasts was one of "hair." (One local station in Boston put a young newscaster through five different changes of hairstyle in a single year.)

More substantively, local television stations began to expand the definition of news by reaching into those areas developed by newspapers and magazines whose hard-news appeal had been lessened by television. Around the country, newspapers and magazines emphasized service features with articles on changing life-styles, how to cope in the modern world, where to find bargains, how to survive in a big city. Newspapers had for many years run "Action Line" columns, helping citizens fight their way through government or corpo-

In direct contrast to the informal news approach is *The MacNeil/Lehrer Report*, shown nightly on the Public Broadcasting System. Reporters Robert MacNeil and Jim Lehrer take one story, using experts in New York and Washington, D.C., and explore that one subject for thirty minutes. Talking heads, complexity, all of the values shunned by most local news broadcasts are permitted here.

rate bureaucracy. Television also made its news departments more feature-oriented, seeking to include the life of the *viewer*, and not just the life of the community, in its broadcasts. Consumer complaints, health tips, advice on bargain shopping, how to "beat the system"—the longer local news programs carried all of these features, and by doing so completed a curious circle. Television news had originally assumed that its strength lay in bringing the viewer to distant places and faraway events, in broadening his horizon. And, after thirty years, it found that a viewer could be reached most powerfully by talking to him about his personal, immediate concerns. It was often effective television, and a useful service. Was it news?

On the network level, the news had been preserved in much the same form for twenty years. In part, this caution was a product of the enormous pressures on network news: from government, with official regulatory power over broadcasting through the FCC, and with great informal power such as that applied by the Nixon administration; from Congress and the courts; and from the endless interest groups that all apparently saw in television an unfair portrayal of their concerns.

To give one example of only one kind of pressure: in addition to the equal time provision of the Federal Communications Act requiring broadcasters to give candidates for public office equal access to air time, the FCC and the courts have imposed a "fairness doctrine" on broadcasting. If a broadcast expresses a viewpoint on a controversial issue, its network or station must present all sides of the argument, not necessarily in the same broadcast, but as part of its overall programming. In theory, this was meant to prevent a licensed government monopoly from turning into a propaganda device. In fact, since few broadcasters want to open up their airwaves to unprofitable public af-

Election Day has meant television vigils since the late 1940s. In this scene *(opposite page, top)* from a 1946 election night, the announcer is shown surrounded by billboard photographs of the candidates. By 1964, Walter Cronkite *(right)* was supported by a more television-conscious studio, as well as the controversial use of computers to predict winners through the use of sample precincts before the total vote was in—and, in some cases, before the polls were closed. The "star" of the 1976 presidential election was NBC's national board *(opposite page, bottom)*, which told the viewer who had carried which states.

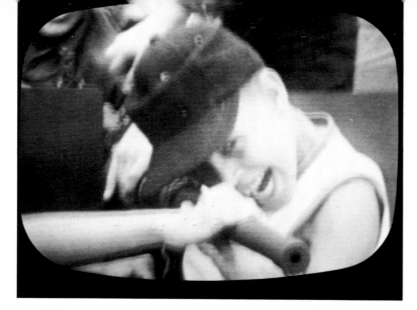

This scene from the controversial CBS documentary "The Selling of the Pentagon" (1971) showed a youngster playing with guns supplied by the Pentagon for public-relations appearances at shopping centers and elsewhere. Charges of distortion led to congressional subpoenas for CBS notes and film; the network refused, and Congress refused to cite the network for contempt.

Barbara Walters, while cohost of *Today*, interviews Henry Kissinger. Her 1976 move to ABC—for a reported salary of a million dollars a year—stirred controversy over mixing news and "personality" on network TV newcasts.

fairs debates, the fairness doctrine resulted in the almost total avoidance of controversial issues. Further, any controversial discussion can produce enormous costs. NBC ran up a six-figure bill defending itself from fairness doctrine proceedings concerning a documentary on pensions. And CBS narrowly avoided a congressional contempt citation for failing to turn over notes and tapes from its 1971 documentary *The Selling of the Pentagon*.

Network caution also arose from strong internal pressure; the people who run the network news operations are fully aware of their power. As one NBC news editor put it, "You have no *idea* how seriously the people here take the news." The "happy talk" specter produced by the success of some local news operations cast a shadow over the networks; no one wanted to take part in making the news informal at the network level. This did not mean, however, that the networks were not contemplating whether they, too, had to begin changing and expanding the definition of news. When Barbara Walters, an interviewer on *Today*, was hired away by ABC to coanchor the evening news, the network's executives intended that move as part of a more general reshaping of the evening news.

"The news viewer," said an executive producer, "is drowning in 'news-speak.' He hears more, and understands less, than ever before." ABC wanted to use a longer network news show—forty-five minutes or an hour—to produce features relating to the viewers' personal concerns: raising children, coping with inflation, surviving a divorce. "News," an ABC executive said, "is not just prescheduled government actions and acts of God. It's what's happening out there, to the man or woman watching the show."

ABC's affiliates strongly opposed a longer news show, however, and the network has retreated to a conventional news format. In the process, it learned that more people were interested in what Harry Reasoner and Barbara Walters thought of each other than in what kind of news show ABC was producing. And, in the spring of 1977, ABC put its sports chief, Roone Arledge, in charge of news as well, a remarkable recognition that modern coverage of news and sports are linked together.

There are other signs that network news is indeed changing, although not on the nightly news shows themselves. In 1968, CBS created a prime-time news magazine show, *60 Minutes*, which won high ratings (in part because it was cleverly programmed against two children's shows). That same network later developed a

Computer animation is used to add visual impact to public affairs programming, as in this graphic for *The Reasoner Report* on ABC.

A long-running public affairs show, *Today*'s cast in 1976 included critic Gene Shalit, host Tom Brokaw, and feature reporter Betty Furness.

The stars of *60 Minutes*—from left, newsmen Morley Safer, Dan Rather, and Mike Wallace—share a laugh with the program's executive producer, Don Hewitt, right.

Live television coverage can still produce memorable images. This photo shows part of the "Operation Sail" pageantry in New York City during the 1976 bicentennial celebration, the highlight of all-day coverage provided by NBC and CBS during the July Fourth festivities.

In an attempt to move away from the New York–Washington, D.C., news monopoly, Charles Kuralt and his CBS "On the Road" crew have been traveling around the country for more than a decade, finding the small, human-interest stories that leaven the network news.

more gossip-oriented prime-time news show, which failed to achieve the ratings success of *60 Minutes*. Both NBC and ABC are in active pursuit of the thriving gossip trade with shows loosely or directly patterned after *People* magazine, which contains interviews with a varied assortment of celebrities and notables.

As with sports, news on television had become a victim of Heisenberg's uncertainty principle of quantum mechanics—in effect, the act of observation changes the object being observed—which seems to be inevitable with an instrument as powerful as television. It was born to observe, but it could not merely observe. Its presence, its technical possibilities, above all its unparalleled capacity to move in "up close and personal" seemed to change whatever it observed. In the process, it also changed the substance of reality. Television was too powerful to bring reality to its viewers; reality was altered in the process beyond recognition.

THE NEXT
GENERATION

Television at the Center ing

If a new generation emerges every thirty years, then television in America—as a mass medium—is about to enter its second generation. Television has been a pervasive national influence since the second half of the twentieth century began; this means that almost every American born since 1948—about 113 million—has never known a world without television. Since its first appearance in the American living room, television's unique power over children has been a source of concern, fear, and outrage. The first warnings about the impact of violent programs on children came in 1950. By 1954, Estes Kefauver, whose Senate investigation of organized crime had done so much to spur sales of television receivers, was holding hearings on the effect of television on younger viewers, and its relation, if any, to rising juvenile delinquency. This concern is still alive today. More than 250 separate studies of television's influence on children have been conducted over the last twenty-five years; the United States Surgeon General found in 1972 a "modest" causal link between televised violence and aggression among children; and the most influential of all TV-watchdog organizations, Action for Children's Television, has organized a strong "citizens' lobby" against televised violence.

But the issue of violence on television, although important, is only one measure of the feared effect of the medium on the younger generation. Television has been blamed for the deterioration in reading and writing skills among the young, as reflected in the steady decline of College Board scores since 1964. It has been blamed for the escalation of violence in the young's criminal behavior. Television has also been blamed for drug use among the young women and men of the 1960s; the shortened attention span of students from elementary school through college; the disintegration of the family.

Buffalo Bob Smith, Howdy Doody, and Clarabell celebrate the tenth anniversary of *Howdy Doody*, the first hit children's show on television. This is a rare moment of quiet in the fast-paced show.

Another early children's show was *Kukla, Fran, and Ollie*, aired first in 1947 and carried East on the newly extended coaxial cable in 1949. Burr Tillstrom was the show's creator (he emerged for this shot), and Fran Allison the only visible grownup. The gentle quality of the show, the absence of screaming children, and the occasional mature observations of Ollie and the other Kuklapolitans built an audience of adults as well as children.

As the children of the television era come to maturity—or at least chronological adulthood—television as a medium is also entering a new generation. Technological possibilities suggest that by the time the second generation of television ends, the average American may well be receiving, and using, television in radically different ways.

How has television changed the generation of Americans now approaching its thirtieth birthday? And what will television be like in its next generation? How will the use of this most powerful of all American institutions alter over the next thirty years? These questions are inseparably linked.

From its first days, television reached out to the young. Even before Milton Berle became known as Mr. Television, *Howdy Doody*, beginning in 1947 on NBC, captivated the kids. The ostensible hero of the show was Howdy Doody (a name that inspired endless school yard scatological jokes), a freckle-faced puppet who told the children to brush their teeth, watch traffic lights, and listen to their parents. The real tension of the show, however, was to be found in the interchange between Buffalo Bob Smith, the good-guy grown-up; the villainous puppet grown-ups (Phineas T. Bluster, The Inspector); and the free spirits, symbolized by the puppet animals (Flubadub) and the androgynous clown Clarabell, with his Harpo Marx horn and his seltzer bottle. (In his freewheeling contempt for grown-up authority, Clarabell may well qualify as America's first Yippie; it was, after all, the *Howdy Doody* audience that grew up into the Berkeley generation.)

Just as adult television shows could be divided into two categories in the early days—the frenetic, New York, show business–based tradition, and the softer, more relaxed, low-pressure approach—so could early children's programs. *Howdy Doody* was a fast-paced show, with a screaming "peanut gallery," slapstick humor, gobs of whipped cream in the face. In contrast, Burr Tillstrom's *Kukla, Fran, and Ollie*, born in Chicago and first telecast on a network basis in 1949, was a quiet, more cerebral show, with a single piano and a single person—Fran Allison (known to other audiences as Aunt Fanny from *Don McNeill's Breakfast Club*)—supporting Tillstrom's "Kuklapolitan" players. The show's characters—including Fletcher Rabbit and Beulah Witch—won a wide following among adults as well as children. The show has remained on television in one form or another almost without interruption; but the spirit and pace of *Kukla, Fran, and Ollie*, as with

Mr. I. Magination and *Captain Kangaroo*, were and are recessive traits. (*Captain Kangaroo*, played from the beginning by Bob Keeshan, who once played Clarabell, is the *only* network children's show broadcast on a daily basis.) Children, no less than adults, are drawn to fast-paced action, and that has been the dominant aspect of children's programming from the beginning.

When a series of old "B" movies starring William Boyd as Hopalong Cassidy surfaced on television in 1948, the white-haired westerner became the first kid-hero of television. *Hopalong Cassidy* sparked a multi-million-dollar merchandising campaign and made the Bar 20 Ranch a fantasy home to millions of children. Cramped television studios became the headquarters for intergalactic space missions, as *Captain Video and His Video Rangers* and *Tom Cor-*

bett, Space Cadet made the real-life astronauts of a decade later seem tame by comparison. For every puppet show with gentle charm and wit—*Time for Beany,* with Stan Freberg helping to make "Cecil the Seasick Sea-Serpent" a beloved figure; Shari Lewis's Lambchop and Charlie Horse—there were a dozen reruns of old serials and westerns, or cartoon shows with inexpensive animation techniques and disturbingly frequent bursts of violent, simplistic action. The Hanna-Barbera partnership, which perfected cheap animation by limiting the moving parts of characters' bodies, created *Huckleberry Hound, Yogi Bear,* and a short-lived prime-time animated show, *The Flintstones*, set in the Stone Age.

There were sporadic attempts to use children's television as an "educational" tool. *Ding Dong School*, with

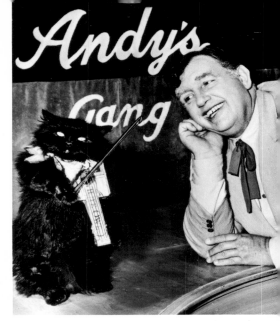

Jack Sterling was ringmaster of *The Big Top*, a Saturday morning circus show out of Philadelphia that was sponsored by Sealtest.

One theory of entertaining children is to act as silly-cute as you think children act. Here Pinky Lee, a lisping, mugging comedian, holds forth on his show of the early 1950s.

Andy Devine succeeded Smilin' Ed McCon in 1957 as host of a Saturday kids' show tha featured a musical duet between Midnight (shown here) and Squeaky, a mouse.

A good example of recycling old movies for television profits is the use of *Our Gang* comedy shorts; these movies have been on television without interruption since the beginning of the medium.

Another movie cowboy who entered television, with *The Roy Rogers Show*, was Roy Rogers, here pointing out the enormous potential profits in film syndication to Dale Evans, Pat Brady, and Nellybelle, the most recalcitrant jeep in the world. Trigger and Buttercup, the stars' horses, are not pictured.

◄ Animals and children; they go together like corned beef and cabbage. *Fury*, a show about a boy and his horse, starred Peter Graves, later of *Mission: Impossible*, as the father, and Bobby Diamond as the boy.

⌐AK⌐

Adam West and Burt Ward starred as the classic comic book crime-fighting duo on *Batman*. The ABC television show of the mid-1960s, presented in high-camp style (with cartoon devices sprinkled into the show), was a short-lived, highly rated fad.

◄ As early as 1951, singing cowboy film star Gene Autry began producing and starring in *The Gene Autry Show*, along with horse Champion in a supporting role. Each week Autry was menaced by the most courteous of hired killers, who would wait until Gene hit the last note of his song before opening fire. Autry is today owner of radio and television properties in California.

First telecast in 1956, *The Wizard of Oz* has become a holiday tradition, shown in its first few years near Christmas, and more recently near Easter. Bert Lahr, Judy Garland, Ray Bolger, and Jack Haley (left to right) starred in the 1939 film whose enduring popularity shows no sign of waning.

◄ In 1949, the radio hero turned television hero and stayed that way until 1960. In *The Lone Ranger*, the *William Tell Overture*, the hyperbolic announcer (". . . a cloud of dust and a hearty 'Hi-Yo, Silver!' "), the respectful master-servant relationship of the Ranger (Clayton Moore) and Tonto (Jay Silverheels) were never-varying constants.

Three preastronaut excursions into science-fiction are shown here. Buzz Corey (middle, left) of the "Spaaaaaace Patrol!" (*left*) played the lead in the early fifties version of a children's radio program. Frankie Thomas was the star of *Tom Corbett, Space Cadet (center)*, set in the twenty-fourth century. Al Hodge was the commander in *Captain Video and His Video Rangers (right)*, a low-budget Du Mont network 1949 presentation.

Dr. Frances Horwich, began in 1952, and *Romper Room*, a franchised show that appears with different teachers in each locality, has been on television since 1953. But the networks saw in children's programming a source of ready profits. By 1965, with Fred Silverman running daytime programming for CBS, the network had shifted its approach toward children. Puppets, old westerns, and educational shows were old hat; children, given a choice between a conventional schoolroom setting and a colorful, fast-paced fantasy world, chose the latter, just as children of earlier generations lined up outside movie theaters on Saturday morning rather than in front of the public library. Children in the mid-1960s were presented with a Saturday morning lineup consisting mainly of first-run cartoons with a heavy reliance on action-adventure and superheroes —in effect, televised comic books. Cartoons, especially with the low cost of animation, were far cheaper than live or filmed shows, since cartoon characters did not have to be paid.

Even better from a commercial point of view, this audience was composed almost entirely of children. For parents seeking a late morning's sleep, Saturday morning television offered a free, constantly available baby-sitter. The advertisers, knowing that their audience was overwhelmingly composed of children twelve years old and under, concocted the most blatant of appeals. Commercials for toys that flew on the screen (but not in the home), foods with high sugar content, dolls and games photographed with the full razzle-dazzle of advertising techniques flooded the morning airwaves. In this area, outside pressure has forced changes; Captain Kangaroo and other children's hosts no longer hawk products on their shows. The amount of advertising in children's programs has been cut back, ending the huge profits from Saturday mornings, although the money spent on children's advertising—$400 million a year—is still considerable.

Violence, always a problem in America, seemed to be growing beyond control in the mid-1960s. It was reflected in the rising crime rates, in riots on college campuses and in cities, in the increasingly angry rhetoric of politics. The Kerner Commission, appointed by President Johnson to investigate the urban riots of the mid-1960s, pointed to the influence of television in highlighting the gap between the material rewards of affluence and the condition of poverty. Within ninety days of the commission's 1968 report, Martin Luther King and Robert Kennedy were assassinated, Washington, D.C., and a dozen other cities were ravaged by

Don Herbert was the wonderful Mr. Wizard, who explained the wonderful world of science to wide-eyed youths on *Mr. Wizard*. Here he demonstrates how to make crystals out of sugar, salt, and other common household materials.

Beginning in 1950, Marlin Perkins, director of the Lincoln Park Zoo in Chicago, was host of *Zoo Parade*, a weekend look at animals. This 1957 photograph was taken at the Bronx Zoo, the setting of two special eighth-anniversary shows.

It wasn't exactly *Sesame Street*, but *Ding Dong School*, which began in 1952 and starred Dr. Frances Horwich, was an early attempt to involve preschool children with learning skills.

riots, and congressional committees and another presidential commission—this one on violence—focused on, among other things, the influence of television on aggressive behavior. This debate, running through the 1972 Surgeon General's report on television violence and extending into a spring, 1977, American Medical Association report urging big corporations to cancel advertising on violence-prone shows, has often been cast in the simplest forms. A child watches *Adam-12*, sees an episode where elderly citizens are attacked, and does the same. A lonely young man sees a television movie about a lonely young man who suddenly goes on a shooting spree, and picks up a rifle to go on his own shooting spree.

This concern—that young minds would see and imitate antisocial behavior on television—spawned one of the television industry's least impressive ideas, the "Family Hour." Launched in the spring of 1975 as an industry code change (it was actually developed through informal and legally questionable dealings between the networks and representatives of the Federal Communications Commission), the Family Hour was

Sid and Marty Krofft became important Saturday children's programmers with *Sigmund and the Sea Monsters*, starring Johnny Whitaker (late of *Family Affair*) and an assortment of friendly monsters.

CBS built a hit Saturday cartoon lineup with shows such as *(above) Scooby Doo, Where Are You?* A more ambitious cartoon effort is *Fat Albert and the Cosby Kids (right)*, based on comic characters created by Bill Cosby; this show attempts to inject some lessons about living in between the comedy.

Hard on the heels of the successful animation of the *Peanuts* company, Dr. Seuss's characters came to television. Shown here are *The Grinch Who Stole Christmas (above)* and *The Cat in the Hat (below)*.

supposedly designed to protect young viewers from the baneful influences of gratuitous sex and violence between the hours of 7 and 9 P.M., Eastern Time. At 9 P.M., as *Variety* put it in a caustic headline, the "gore curtain" would rise, and police dramas, with their gunplay and fistfights, could commence. For reasons of network scheduling, the "Family Hour" ended at 8 P.M. local time in the Midwest; this was justified by one FCC functionary on the grounds that children in the Midwest go to bed earlier than their Eastern counterparts. The fact that the Nielsen surveys showed that 10.8 million children under the age of eleven were still watching television at nine o'clock, or that three million youths under the age of seventeen were still watching at *midnight,* gave one clue to the futility of the Family Hour. In its first season, the Family Hour diluted the content of such sophisticated, high-quality shows as *M*A*S*H** and *Barney Miller*—another of its shortcomings. Most important, the way the Family Hour was created—by pressure on the industry from the Congress and the FCC rather than by formal legislation or rule making—rendered it unlawful, according to a 1976 opinion by a California federal court.

In terms of the real impact of television on children, however, the Family Hour was aimed at the edge of the target, not the bull's-eye. For what researchers were finding was less a direct correlation between television and violence than a correlation between a childhood spent in front of a television set and patterns in learning and development. The essential facts as gathered by the A. C. Nielsen Company, which measures audience size, characteristics, and attitudes for the television industry, are these: the youngest television viewers, those under five, watch 23.5 hours of television a week. Extended over a child's first eighteen years, that means 15,000 hours of watching television—as compared with 11,000 hours of schooling. It means that the disparate diversions of pretelevision childhood—the Saturday morning movie, the after-school comic book, the weekend trip to the ball park, the adventure novel—are all supplied by a flick of the switch. It means a "window on the world" that presents a world of quick cuts, pervasive action, fragmented information. In 1963, social critic Paul Goodman observed of children's television programs, "They are jumpy and fragmented. They are strangled by a format imposed on them to hold them together as an identifiable package. They create anxiety by their haste and greedy crowding of every second. . . . They try too hard for fun and sensation rather than allowing beauty and feeling to breathe and happen."

Product of the most ambitious and expensive effort to use television to teach learning skills and social values, *Sesame Street* has been running on (mostly) public television stations since 1969. The real-life actors and the Muppets represent the kind of people children meet and the kind of emotional states children pass through; Big Bird *(right)*, for instance, is the child who never quite understands what is going on. Above is the entire *Sesame Street* cast of 1977.

This format was inherent in the most ambitious effort to design a different kind of children's television, *Sesame Street.* It was created by the Children's Television Workshop in 1969 after years of study. Financial support came from the Ford Foundation, the U.S. Office of Education, and the Carnegie Corporation, giving *Sesame Street* an annual budget of $8 million in its first three years, and $5 million thereafter. The series was a worthy attempt to reach the less verbally skilled children, especially those belonging to minority groups, with a show that could teach basic elements of cognitive skills through visually arresting devices. Tests on children had shown a resistance to slow-

Mr. Rogers' Neighborhood, created by and starring psychologist Fred Rogers as the friendly, undemanding neighbor ("I like you just the way you are") was a hard show for some parents to like; but children seemed to trust this easygoing personality (he's shown here with Mr. McFeely from the Speedy Delivery Company, played by David Newell). The show, which ended new production in 1976 but was still shown in reruns, was very careful to avoid the hard-action slapstick fantasy that Rogers saw as a case of adults "dipping into their own unresolved childhood fantasies. . . ."

Zoom!, another PBS show, was a different kind of kids' show, with children, exclusively, performing in front of the camera. Children at home sent in games, jokes, and stories, and filmed pieces dealt with unusually skilled children.

paced shows such as *Captain Kangaroo*. Instead, *Sesame Street* deliberately employed the devices of commercials and entertainment shows, particularly the kind of techniques used by *Laugh-In*. Quick, short bursts of entertaining and informative "lessons," running gags, a mixture of cartoons, Muppet characters, live actors, and film—all were designed to keep the child's attention while number skills, the alphabet, concepts such as "near and far" or "high and low" were communicated to the audience.

The superiority of *Sesame Street* and its progeny, such as *The Electric Company,* to conventional children's programming was and is undeniable. But what effect did this process of information transmittal have on the television generation? Did it matter that the pace of television—with rare exceptions such as *Mr. Rogers' Neighborhood* and *Captain Kangaroo*—was frenetic? That there were few silences? That ideas were presented quickly, broken off, picked up again out of linear sequence? Writer Michael Novak, after teaching members of the television generation, noted that "one may swiftly change the subject, shift the scene, drop a line of argument in order to pick it up later—and not lose the logic of development." The more formal, sequential kind of teaching, he reported, did not seem to work. A 1977 *Newsweek* article quoted a Maryland first-grade teacher: "You introduce a new skill, and right away, if it looks hard, they dissolve into tears. They want everything to be easy—like watching the tube."

About the more general effects of a generation,s obsession with television, it is impossible to be precise. It is possible only to look at the fundamental ways in which this generation has changed from its forebears, and match those changes against the likely impact due to their spending more time watching television than on any other single pursuit save sleep.

• We know that the reading habits of this generation have changed; College Board scores show a steady decline in the reading comprehension of prospective college students. Also, the so-called "New Journalism," which moved away from the neutral, dispassionate reporting of wire-service journalism in favor of highly charged, personal observations of the effect of an event or a public figure on the *writer,* is gaining popularity.

• This generation is more openly committed to private gratification than its predecessors; the conventional path of maturity is ignored by growing numbers of Americans. Studies of 1977 show a growing pattern: men and women are delaying marriages, delaying or abandoning the idea of having children, and, most surprising, are living alone for much longer periods. When television became a national fact of American life in 1950, one of the primary concerns of America was how to find the schools to educate the children of the baby boom. A quarter of a century later, the birth rate in America was well below zero population growth.

• The political and institutional loyalties of Americans have weakened and frayed; political participation has dwindled as well. Since 1948, there has been, with the single exception of the 1964 presidential election, a steady decline in the percentage of Americans exercising their franchise in choosing the most powerful figure in the country. And a steady decline in public confidence, not just in government, but in every institution from business to labor to medicine to religion to science, has marked the coming of age of the television generation.

To blame, or credit, television for these trends would be inane. After World War II, America underwent a wholesale, radical change of life: from blue collar to white collar, from cultural conservatism to cultural relativism, from city and small town to homogeneous suburbanism, from the shotgun marriage to the pill. And much of the growth of cynicism in American society can be traced, not to the existence of television, but to television's direct, unavoidable presence, in living rooms and bedrooms, as a messenger of news. However much television news can itself be faulted—

for its celebration of frenetic action, for its obsession with the instant trends and sudden celebrities of public life—it did not make up police dogs and fire hoses, napalm in Vietnam, dissembling and corruption up to and including the highest levels of government.

As to the concern about children and the violent, aggressive world they frequently see on television, the studies so far suggest the problem is less a direct triggering of violence among TV watchers and more a problem of *indifference* to violence against others. Sociologist Leo Bogart, writing of a 1975 study, says that the problem is not that when a child sees someone shooting a gun on television he will reach for a gun himself. Instead, says Bogart, the child will conclude "the world is a wicked and hostile place in which one must aggressively protect oneself."

"The really great impact of media violence," Bogart continues, "on our own culture may arise mainly from this diffuse raising of the general public level of anxiety rather than from individual acts of behavior in response to individual media episodes or instances." A Mississippi psychologist concluded from a more recent study, "Television desensitizes children to violence in real life. They tolerate violence in others because they have been conditioned to think of it as an everyday thing."

It is more than likely that the sheer magnitude of time spent by the first television generation in front of that device may have helped to spur a growth of indiscriminate cynicism. Many of television's critics worry that it is creating a generation of "zombies," staring slack-jawed at the screen, obeying the advertisements as so many automatons. But every generation grows up to learn that its elders distort, avoid, and lie; in the case of this generation, that insight has come from the same source as its dominant diversion: television. From the quiz show scandals of the late 1950s to the political upheavals of the next decade, and reinforced throughout by the dishonesty of the television commercials that promised wonders the products did not deliver, this generation has learned not to trust what it sees on television. And since so much of what it sees of life is seen through television, some of the lack of anchoring belief afflicting many of the young may be traced to the experience of relying so heavily on a medium that casually, inevitably mixes high tragedy with the most blatant of untruths—that can, in a matter of seconds, switch from a family or a nation enveloped in grief to a blithering idiot enveloped in grease. When Thomas Beaver, professor of psychology at Columbia University, studied youngsters from the ages of five to

While the Picture Phone never caught on, the future is likely to see more of this kind of telephone-video hook-up: using push-button telephones to "punch up" bank balances, inventories, price lists.

twelve, he found that their disenchantment with dishonest television commercials did not stop at distrust in advertising. Said Beaver, "They become ready to believe that, like advertising, business and other institutions are riddled with hypocrisy." That study, it can be argued, may overlook the fact that "business and other institutions" *are* riddled with hypocrisy. But the dilemma remains: if children learn that what is on television is not true, then they are, in effect, learning that every American institution is dishonest. That is a dispiriting vision to carry into maturity.

What kind of television will the next generation be watching? Even before it was perfected, television was considered a device of limitless possibilities. It has been seen as a way of communicating by vision as well as sound (although, outside of being used in a few privileged offices in Nixon's White House, the Picture Phone never did catch on), as a way of linking viewers with the marketplace and public officials (although President Carter's first people-to-people communications experiment was done on radio, not on television), as another means of ending the isolation and sense of powerlessness of ordinary citizens (although, overwhelmingly, television produces a sense of passivity). Until recently, the only major technological breakthrough enjoyed by the average viewer was color television. However, it is apparent that a number of other television uses will soon be as available to the general public as was TV itself at the start of the 1950s. All of them promise to expand the use of the medium. And all of them both reflect and reinforce the central position of television in the American experience.

One such change already beginning to have an effect is cable television. Ironically, cable repudiates the most exciting aspect of broadcasting, the ability to send voices and images through the air. Cable television, in this sense, is not broadcasting at all. Instead, signals go from a transmitter through a series of microwave relays and closed circuit lines through underground coaxial cables directly into the receivers at home, and the viewer pays a charge for this service. Cable TV was originally intended as nothing more than a means of linking faraway broadcast signals to homes in isolated communities. It actually began, in limited fashion, with radio, when a Dundee, Michigan, entrepreneur built such an antenna in 1923, charging listeners $1.50 a month for a hookup. In 1948, the FCC imposed a three-year freeze on new station licenses in order to prevent massive interference with television signals, and. to organize the general chaos spawned by the coming of television and the huge demand for television licenses. Since no new stations went. on the air from 1948 to 1951, this meant that many smaller communities, far away from then-existing television stations, could not receive broadcast signals. So giant antennas that could pick up signals from stations hundreds of miles away were built; these antennas were linked by cable to viewers for a fee. This is why cable television originally came to be known as CATV—Community Antenna Television.

It was soon realized, however, that there were other advantages to cable TV besides good, clear reception. When the Dodgers moved from Brooklyn to Los Angeles, their owner decided to avoid the curse of televised home games, which reduce attendance, by selling rights to home games through Subscription Television. Other cable TV operators realized that the cable broke through the limits of broadcasting; instead of the maximum of seven VHF stations that can be sent through the air, a single cable could carry as many as eighty different signals into a home television receiver.

A contemporary vision of an unlikely future is RCA's prototype cylindrical console with twin screens. Perfect for watching two football games, or further atomizing the family.

Basic Cable Television System

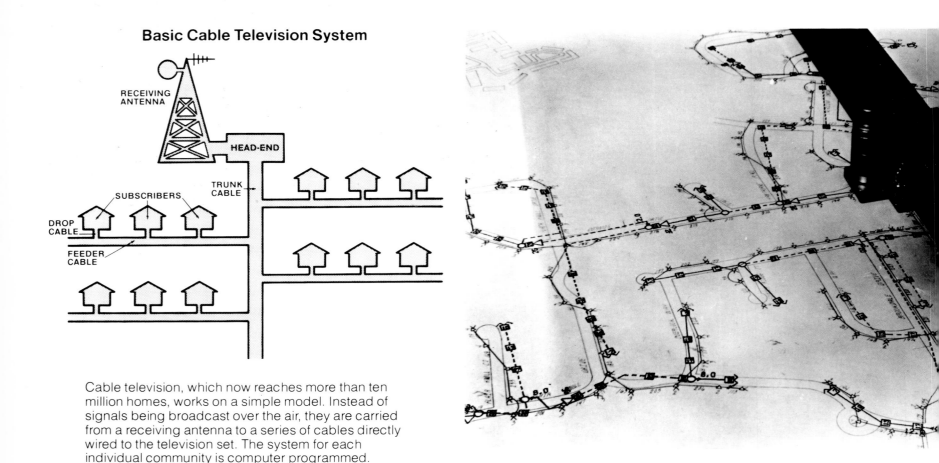

Cable television, which now reaches more than ten million homes, works on a simple model. Instead of signals being broadcast over the air, they are carried from a receiving antenna to a series of cables directly wired to the television set. The system for each individual community is computer programmed.

And the closed-circuit nature of the operation meant that a relatively small number of viewers, paying for what the general public could not receive, could supply huge revenues to show producers and movie makers, who could then sell the same program to a broadcast station or network. For example, a half-hour program costing $200,000 to produce could be supported by a television network paying a license fee—or it could be supported by two million people paying ten cents apiece, or two hundred thousand people paying a dollar apiece in return for a program unavailable on regular TV. In other words, the audience could be select rather than mass.

This possible alternative to broadcasting was not greeted kindly by existing station and network owners. They rightly saw in cable television an eventual end to their outsized profits once viewers were given the choice of twenty, fifty, or eighty different programs rather than three or four. Movie-theater owners also saw in cable television, with its economic base permitting the purchase of first-run movies, a new threat to

their lifeblood. Despite their combined efforts—an early pay-television system was outlawed in California by a statewide vote in 1964—cable television continued to grow. And with it grew *pay* television. This phrase covers a multitude of systems: viewers can receive special programs broadcast over the air, which requires a special "unscrambler" attached to a set; or they can pay for each program, whether broadcast or transmitted by cable; or, in the most typical arrangement, they can pay an extra monthly fee for a special cable channel that shows first-run films, sports events, and other special entertainment.

Cable television, according to A. C. Nielsen Company figures, in 1977 reached more than ten million American homes—more than 14 percent of all American television households. In some cities, it operates under franchises requiring it to set aside channels and equipment for "public access"—a throwback to the early radio concept of "toll booth" broadcasting, except that here the use of facilities and air time is free. Anyone who wants to—boy scouts, vegetarians, folk dancers, community activists, political outsiders—can get about a half hour of air time a week through the facilities of a cable television company. This "public-access" concept is still in its infancy; equipment and lighting is poor, sound is sometimes weak, and programs often reflect total amateurishness. But public-access programming shows that, with a cable system, the perennial television problem of scarcity is eased. The same television set can accommodate all commercial and public broadcast channels, plus a pay-TV channel, plus public broadcast channels, plus wire services, plus consumer price lists, plus telecasts of blacked-out sports events. With a recent court decision freeing cable television from many FCC-imposed restrictions on what kinds of movies and programs can be shown on a cable system, it is clear that this device represents a major area of growth. One communications professional estimates that by the end of the twentieth century, cable—not broadcasting—will be the way American viewers receive their television programs.

Another kind of change in the use of television is the growing capacity of the viewer to program for himself, through a device that allows him to see what he wants, when he wants it. Although this invention is still in its early stages, it will probably emerge as a major alternative to conventional television. Already being marketed is the Sony Betamax, a small cassette device that records television programs, either while the viewer is out of the house or while he is watching a separate program broadcast at the same time, and plays them back at the viewer's convenience. This system is less bulky than existing playback systems, and there are indications that viewers are using the Betamax system not just to record and play back shows, but to build their own library of favorite shows and movies (two major movie studios are suing to ban this practice).

A more elaborate version of the viewer-as-programmer (and one that does not raise the bootlegging issue, where viewers record and then sell movies illegally) is electronic video recording, soon to be released to the public. First presented as a workable system by Peter Goldmark, then president of CBS Laboratories, in 1968, EVR is a kind of phonograph for television. A film cassette is inserted into a player, and a movie, theatrical performance, lecture, concert, or famous sports event is played on a home television screen. It has been predicted for years that this device will exert a major influence on viewing patterns, since it

These pictures show two important uses of the computer in television. Computer animation *(top)*, as executed by Dolphin Studios in New York, has made possible the remarkable color graphics that introduce sporting events, network promotions, and many advertising campaigns. Another application of computer art *(above)* is in captioning shows for the hard-of-hearing through a process developed by the Public Broadcasting System. Shows can be run with or without the captions. Here, Bill Bixby narrates *Once Upon a Classic*.

The Sony Betamax uses small video cassettes to record programs, either while the viewer is out of the house or while two programs he wants to see are on at the same time.

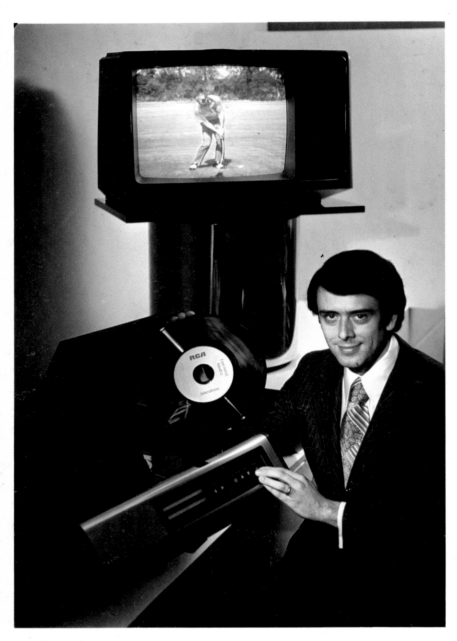

The video disc, this one by RCA, has been heralded as the wave of the future; it enables the viewer to see movies, shows, anything that can be prerecorded, at his own time and choosing. At present, the marketing of incompatible systems poses a major threat to this new use of television.

frees the viewer from dependency on a television station's schedule. But there are problems. Just as color television could not be marketed until there was one exclusively used receiving system, EVR may not succeed unless the competing companies develop a compatible system for playing these video cassettes or video discs. In 1977, at least two major marketing concerns plan to introduce EVR systems that are incompatible; both have bought the rights to different motion picture and theatrical attractions. Whether this expensive system will succeed—especially with the less complicated home video recorders already on the market—is problematical.

Actually, the American viewer is already doing his own television programming, although not in the manner described by prophets of major innovations. In 1977, approximately 7 million home video games will have been sold. These devices are simple computer games which, when attached to television terminals, provide electronic versions of hockey, soccer, and tennis. In one sense, the device represents an alternative to the passivity of receiving programs broadcast by others. In another sense, it represents the enormous hold television has on Americans, since even their playtime diversions have moved out of the playground or game room and into the cathode-ray tube.

There are a wide range of "alternative" television possibilities beyond these few. Public television, so long starved for funds, is now a genuine, if still junior, fourth network. It aims to draw the largest audience possible by providing alternatives to commercial programs, particularly in the area of news and public affairs. It is willing to satisfy viewers who desire longer discussions of public affairs, although such programs contain little visual interest. At the other end of the scale of values, giant-screen home television has become a reality. The Advent Company markets screens six and seven feet, measured diagonally (the picture comes from a floor-mounted projector). Sony has developed a device to turn home movies and slides into pictures that can be shown on a television set. And at least one cable company in the Midwest is experimenting with two-way television—at least to the extent of permitting viewers to order products displayed on the screen by pushing a button. With the growing use of minicomputers, it is possible to imagine a near future in which bank balances, prices, and other information can be obtained through a cable television hooked up to a push-button telephone.

What every one of these devices has in common, of course, is that they concede the centrality of television

The Advent VideoBeam (a projector mounted on the floor beams the television picture onto a lightweight seven-foot screen, measured diagonally) made giant home television a possibility for those with $4,000 or so to spare. Note the pictorial implication of sophistication and communal participation—just as in ads for early television sets.

A 1963 experiment in marketing by television was tried in a Tucson apartment complex; this closed-circuit device also enabled apartment dwellers to watch their children, see visitors in the lobby, and learn the weather reports. It did not catch on.

Television is everywhere; here a closed-circuit system in a supermarket offers prizes to shoppers who can identify three advertised products—and perhaps stimulates impulse buying.

A vision of shopping by giant television is presented in this Walt Disney World futuristic home. A worldwide credit card can be used to order anything displayed on the screen, thus making it possible to plunge into massive debt with a touch of a button.

RCA is not the name of a new space-age nation; this is *(left)* the launching of an early 1960s Communications Satellite, which made instantaneous worldwide audio and visual communications a reality. One of the uses of satellite television was this 1965 Parke-Bernet auction *(above)*. A New York audience, linked to London's Sotheby showroom by satellite transmission, could bid on paintings displayed an ocean away.

in American society. This fact is deplored by some, accepted by others. But it is not going to go away. The Roper Organization, which has been polling for the television industry since the 1950s, reports a steadily increasing acceptance of television—of its news, its programming, its financial system in which sponsors pay for the programs. Apart from a strong concern among parents' groups and some major corporations with violence on television, Americans seem to have placidly accepted what television is, what it does, what it offers them.

It is therefore not surprising that, as television moves into its second generation, all of the plans for its future are based on the premise that television will continue to be the dominant force in the nonworking life of the American people. It may grow bigger, more diverse. Viewers may use it on their own time, to play favorite stories and programs; they may even use it to market and transact personal finances. But the more people attempt to reshape the face of television, the more they give silent assent to the fact that it will continue to be central to their lives. And the first television generation will have to contend for its children's attention with a medium more powerful, appealing, and attractive than that which its parents had to compete with almost thirty years ago.

Bibliography

Literally thousands of books and countless articles have been written about broadcasting over the last half-century. What follows is a list of those books which may prove of interest to the general reader with a desire to learn more about the television industry.

Arlen, Michael. *Living-Room War.* New York: Viking, 1969.
———. *The View from Highway 1.* New York: Farrar, Straus & Giroux, 1976.
   Two collections of television criticism by the resident television viewer of *The New Yorker.*

Barnouw, Erik. *A History of Broadcasting in the United States.* New York: Oxford. Vol. 1: *A Tower in Babel: To 1933,* 1966; Vol. 2: *The Golden Web: 1933 to 1953,* 1968; Vol. 3: *The Image Empire: From 1950,*1970.
   This three-volume account is the definitive history of broadcasting in America. It combines scholarship with first-rate writing. A one-volume condensation of the television material, *Tube of Plenty,* was published in 1975.

Brown, Les. *Television: The Business Behind the Box.* New York: Harcourt Brace Jovanovich, 1971.
   Brown, who reports on television for the *New York Times,* wrote this account of the television industry while covering the business for *Variety.* A closeup view of one season's ratings wars, the book also gives an excellent overview of how commercial television works.

Efron, Edith. *The News Twisters.* Los· Angeles: Nash Publishing, 1971.
   A view from the conservative end of the political spectrum of how networks manipulate the news.

Epstein, Edward J. *News from Nowhere: Television and the News.* New York: Random House, 1973.
   An examination of network television news which challenges assumptions of the industry and many of its critics by focusing on the structural pressures on broadcast news operations.

Everson, George. *The Story of Television: The Life of Philo T. Farnsworth.* New York: Norton, 1949.
   The story of one of the inventors most responsible for modern television.

Friendly, Fred W. *Due to Circumstances Beyond Our Control . . .* New York: Random House, 1967.
   The former president of CBS News, who resigned over the network's refusal to cover a Senate hearing on Vietnam, writes about the tensions in broadcast news and other pressures on the commercial networks.

Greenfield, Jeff. *No Peace, No Place.* Garden City, N.Y.: Doubleday, 1973.
   One chapter focuses on the early days of television, suggesting that television became a peephole through which the younger generation viewed the hypocrisies of its elders.

Johnson, Nicholas. *How to Talk Back to Your Television Set.* Boston: Little, Brown, 1970.
   The former maverick Federal Communications Commissioner offers an antiestablishment view of broadcasting, and suggests how citizens can organize to put pressure on the industry.

Kendrick, Alexander. *Prime Time: The Life of Edward R. Murrow.* Boston: Little, Brown, 1969.
   A biography of broadcasting's most outstanding journalist, this book also recounts many of the battles between CBS News and other divisions within CBS.

MacNeil, Robert. *The People Machine.* New York: Harper & Row, 1968.
   A perceptive look at television's effects on politics and attitudes.

Mayer, Martin. *About Television.* New York: Harper & Row, 1972.
   A veteran magazine writer offers a collection of pieces about different aspects of television, from prime-time program production to sports. An excellent way to learn a great deal while being entertained.

Metz, Robert. *CBS: Reflections in a Bloodshot Eye.* Chicago: Playboy Press, 1975.
   An irreverent anecdotal account of the rise of CBS and the life of CBS chief William S. Paley.

Mickelson, Sig. *Electric Mirror: Politics in an Age of Television.* New York: Dodd, Mead, 1972.
   This prominent network news executive offers a clear view of news from the inside. Whether you agree with him or not, his book is a valuable guide to the way television news is perceived by those who produce it.

Miller, Merle, and Rhodes, Evan. *Only You, Dick Daring.* New York: Sloane, 1964.
   A very funny, very cynical view of Miller's loss of innocence when he wrote a television pilot for CBS during the network presidency of James Aubrey.

Shanks, Bob. *The Cool Fire: How to Make It in Television.* New York: Norton, 1976.
   Shanks, a veteran of the television wars, has written an indispensable guide for the student who wants to make television a career. It describes the way television works, what jobs exist, and—with a wealth of stories—the way up the ladder in the industry. Often cynical, it is also important as an eye-opening dose of realism for the would-be television impresario.

Shayon, Robert Lewis. *The Crowd-Catchers: An Informal Introduction to Television.* New York: Saturday Review Press, 1973.
   A thought-provoking, highly useful guide to the medium. Shayon, a longtime writer for and about television, has ways of looking at the industry that are original and absorbing.

Shulman, Arthur, and Youman, Roger. *How Sweet It Was.* New York: Shorecrest, 1966.
   A remarkable collection of some 1,500 photographs of television shows during the first twenty years of commercial programming. A useful source for settling arguments.

Winn, Marie. *The Plug-In Drug: Television, Children, and the Family.* New York: Viking Press, 1976.
   A polemic against children's excessive reliance on television, *regardless of the content.* Whether the program is *The Flintstones* or *Sesame Street,* Winn argues, watching television is a passive, unhealthy activity. She suggests ways of convincing children—and grown-ups—to cut down.

Index

*Numbers in **boldface** refer to the pages on which the illustrations appear.*
Asterisks (*) denote colorplates.

Photographic Credits

The author and publisher would like to thank the organizations listed below for supplying the necessary photographs and for permitting their reproduction in this book. All numbers refer to pages on which the photographs are found. Individual photographers are noted in parentheses following the page listing.

ABC: 13 (Heinz Kluetmeier), 121, 205, 224, 228 (Heinz Kluetmeier), 241, 242 (George Long); Advent Corporation: 272; American Stock Photos: 14; Atari: 271; N. W. Ayer ABH International: 174; Bara, Nina: 258; The Bettmann Archive Inc.: 30, 86, 258; Black Star: 10, 11; Leo Burnett U.S.A.: 171, 177, 183, 184–85, 186, 187; CBS: 41, 46, 53, 54, 54–55, 55, 56, 64, 65, 67, 68, 69, 70, 71, 72, 73, 77, 78, 81, 82, 85, 89, 96, 100, 104, 107, 108, 109, 110, 111, 113, 114, 115, 116, 117, 118, 119, 120, 121, 122, 124, 125, 126, 128, 130, 131, 132, 134, 138, 139, 140, 144, 145, 146, 149, 151, 152, 154, 157, 158, 159, 162, 173, 192, 193, 195, 197, 200, 201, 202, 203, 205, 210, 211, 213, 215, 216, 217, 218, 219, 220, 225, 226, 229, 237, 241, 245, 246, 247, 248, 250, 255, 256, 260, 261; CBS News: 20, 22, 45, 230, 231, 232, 234, 235, 236, 238; CBS Radio: 199; Children's Television Workshop: 262, 263, Dick Clark Enterprises: 15; Clio Magazine: 170, 172, 174, 176, 178, 180, 182, 185, 187; Compton Advertising Inc.: 169; Cossette, Pierre: 84; Culver Pictures: 37; Dolphin Productions, Inc.: 27, 249, 269; Exxon Corporation: 50; Family Communications Inc.: 264; Four D Productions: 115; Group W: 76, 81; Hunstein, Don: 225; Michals, Duane: 10; More Magazine: 168, 181; National Cable Television Association: 268; NBC: 16, 21, 23, 24, 26, 40, 47, 57, 63, 69, 70, 71, 72, 72–73, 74, 75, 79, 81, 82, 83, 84, 85, 86, 87, 88, 90, 91, 92, 93, 94, 95 (Paul W. Bailey), 96–97, 97, 98, 99, 100, 102, 103, 105, 112, 117, 121, 122, 123, 133, 142, 143, 144, 149, 150, 151, 153, 155, 156, 159, 160, 161, 194, 195, 196, 198, 203, 204, 210, 210–11, 211, 214, 215, 216, 221, 222–23, 232, 232–33, 240, 247, 248, 250, 256, 257, 259; © Paramount Pictures Corporation: 147; PBS: 163, 264, 269; Peck, Charles: 11; Prentice-Hall, Inc.: 32; Python U.S.: 87; RCA: 19, 32, 33, 34, 40, 42, 43, 44, 47, 270, 273, 274; RCA News: 267; Rogers & Cowan Inc.: 50; Scali, McCabe, Sloves, Inc.: 183; Schwerin, Ron: 252–53; Smithsonian Institution: 31; Sony Corporation of America: 269; Spelling/Goldberg Productions: 148, 153, 208; Stokey, Mike: 195; © Copyright 1977 Tandem Productions, Inc. All rights reserved: 54 (Maude), 112 (All in the Family); © Copyright 1977 T.A.T. Communications Co. All rights reserved: 54 (Jeffersons), 206 (Mary Hartman, Mary Hartman); © Time Inc.: 76 (Michael Mauney, Life Magazine); Twentieth Century-Fox Television: 206; United Artists Television: 121, 156; Universal/MCA: 138, 144, 148, 153; UPI: 18, 21, 25, 36, 39, 41, 45, 142, 198, 212, 226, 258, 272, 273; Volkswagen of America, Inc.: 188; Welk Productions: 53; Western Electric Company, Inc.: 266; Wide World Photos, Inc.: 15, 17, 18, 28, 34, 37, 46, 70, 135, 217, 220, 227, 235, 236, 239, 240, 242–43, 243, 244, 254, 272; Wisconsin Center for Film and Theatre Research: 62, 63, 66, 71, 74, 106, 107, 109, 121, 126, 146, 150, 259; WNET-Channel 13, New York: 207, 246 (Carl Samrock); David Wolper Productions: 58–59, 110, 159, 165; WTTG-TV, Washington, D.C.: 190.